MARTHA RENEE

BOOK 2

CLAUDETTE MCLENNON

EXPLORA BOOKS
700 – 838 West Hastings St. Vancouver
BC V6C 0A6
www.explorabooks.com
Phone: (604) 330 6795

No part of this book may be reproduced, stored in a retrieval system, or transmitted by any means without the written permission of the author.

Because of the dynamic nature of the Internet, any web addresses or links contained in this book may have changed since publication and may no longer be valid. The views expressed in this work are solely those of the author and do not necessarily reflect the views of the publisher, and the publisher hereby disclaims any responsibility for them.

ISBN: 978-1-83430-098-6 *(Paperback)*
978-1-83430-122-8 *(Hardback)*
978-1-83430-099-3 *(eBook)*

© 2025 Claudette H. Mclennon. All rights reserved.

MARTHA RENEE

BOOK 2

CLAUDETTE MCLENNON

Dedication

In memory of my family and close friends; I cherish fond memories of your encouragement, belief in me, faith that I'd accomplish my dreams and to craft a worthwhile legacy to inspire and motivate others.

Table of Contents

Dedication i
Preface v
Chapter 1 7
Chapter 2 11
Chapter 3 37
Chapter 4 65
Chapter 5 75
Chapter 6 83
Chapter 7 97
Chapter 8 127
Chapter 9 157
Epilogue 177
Acknowledgement 179
About the Author 181

Preface

Martha is cleared by DNA of the murder of Judge Earl Frontes. She has done TV interviews and declines multiple offers to host a talk show. She has to fight depression as she struggles to assimilate back in society, finds ten years' incarceration is marathon. Can she go back to WASP? How will her new found faith in Christ shadow her future. Can she reclaim her son stolen at birth. Can she find her daughter, his twin. She wants to live for Christ but she must seek forgiveness from her parents and children. The ministry beckons but can she make it. And her biggest temptation Adrian Boone. Can she resist him without compromise. Can she reunite her family?

Chapter 1

Martha stayed with Nana. At the end of three months, had three television interviews, including one with The View. She was surprised how ordinary and cordial the group was. They were not intimidating. They were normal. The irrepressible Joy and outrageous Whoopi made her feel right at home. They asked relevant questions about life at Bedford Hill and changes since she got there. What did she do? She explained not much but rather encouraged the ladies who didn't complete high school to do the GED. She also asked for creative outlet. Many are talented artists, hence plea for art supplies. She negotiated that if funds were found then the paintings could be sold for reimbursement. She advocated for speakers other than psychiatrists to visit and give talks on being entrepreneurs. She pushed for toiletries other than soap. They were women that were a wiz with a comb, could replicate any style. They did braids, twists, buns. This was the plea for when their children and mothers visited. She pushed for better food and nutrition.

Whoopi asked her how she kept her sanity. With a grim smile, she said it wasn't easy. She used her mind to anticipate freedom and what she would do when she was out. At the onset, she was viewed as a Yuppie and targeted for a beating. She was beaten, got a cracked rib and was in the infirmary for a week. She knew the attackers but never said. She said she was attacked from behind, which was true and most of the time was lying face down. She was kicked in the side. She pretended to be knocked out. With blood coming from her nose and a gash in her head, they left her. Somebody called the guards after and she was taken to the hospital, then discharged to the infirmary. Of course, no one did it. It was a harsh, hostile environment. After that, she worked out every day. She did planks, push-ups, and sit-ups. I watched Billy Blank. She was busy staying alive and waiting to be exonerated. She was unfortunate to get a quack for an attorney who didn't work for her release. But I was confident that I would not be convicted because it was all circumstantial. Two of my friends testified we were together, only separated to see who could reach the restaurant first, by taking different routes on foot. I screamed and this man came, and I told him to get help. Yes, but I was not thinking when I rushed the person and here is the scar on my hand, I used to protect my chest and face but not even realizing I was bleeding too, I bent over the judge. You know, in my sober moments, days later; all I could think, what a waste. A tear escaped the corner of her eye. What she did not say was for all that brilliant legal mind, handsome, gorgeous male specimen he was, his one weakness destroyed him.

She explained she started a book club and revived the literacy program. Many of the inmates joined the literacy program and passed the GED. For the accomplishment they had a graduation. Many persons there are just misguided, made bad choices, influenced by friends or victims of circumstances and the abysmal failure of role models. There are lot of social issues that got them there. Thus, she wants to invest in teenagers to do voluntary work at counseling centers. There should be emphasis on prevention rather than applying the cure after the fact. She doesn't have the answers or pretends that she has but is willing to team up with a social group. She believes outreach from schools and churches can impact these children. It is necessary to have after-school programs; so, they can channel their energies, desires and talents.

Martha was restless and listless. She opened WhatsApp and heard Miss Landle singing. The God of The Mountain Is Still the God in The Valley. She played it repeatedly. She needs that assurance and reminder. She's happy Denise sent it to her. Her baby sister is an ardent Christian and is engaged to a seminary student. Thinking of her baby sister puts a smile on her lips. She realized getting back to normal isn't really normal or easy. She has to fight depression. And she knows her walk with the Divine should be just that as she is not interested in religion. She picks up her Bible and turns to the 23rd Psalm, alternately singing it and reading it. Then she reads Psalm 121. She needs a lot of help. It seems she cannot find a niche. She will go back to Colombia, to Divinity school. That may bring her some focus, direction and peace of mind. If fully immersed in the Word and learning and understanding the scriptures, then she believes her way will be clarified for her. The next scripture that pops in her head is the prayer of Jabez. Thank you, Google, she says softly as she finds First Chronicles 4 verses 9 and 10. She prays for mercy, peace and contentment. With some decisions settled, her spirit picks up.

As she contemplates taking the plunge of giving NYU Medical Center another chance, she realizes it's wishful thinking. Somehow it becomes clearer that a big part of her restlessness is NYU medical Centre. She does not want to go there. Personnel called Charlotte to get her number and offered her a job. Martha wonders if the offer is motivated by guilt. She chides herself for being cynical and looking a gift horse in the mouth as Nana said. She does not want to be anyone's charity case, but she'd go in and see personal director Yvonne Stone. If one is an institution, she must have come with the building. Martha smiles at her thoughts. Anyway, she'll go but needs a suit. But from what she sees, most people don't appear to wear suits. But she realizes television is not necessarily the best guide there. However, what does it matter anyway? She may not accept the offer if it conflicts with school.

So, she accepts the invitation as a genuine offer and goes. This time is unlike the time before. Last time it was to wow the interviewer. Navy blue suit with a scarf disguised as a blouse, folded and pleated in front, two inches high heels, black sheer stockings, manicured nails and hair pulled back in a bun, neat. Yes, she was ready to conquer the world. Everything, said confidence, her makeup understated, enhanced and didn't detract. Good old Mary Kay! The Mary Kay ladies made you want to wear makeup. Martha smiles and comes back to the present. She loves the 3D miracle set and foundation and silky setting powder. She is not conceited, but Mary Kay Color Cosmetics loves her. In a changing world Mary Kay remains constant and reliable. It's just like her WASP girlfriends.

The interview is a formality. She is offered her old job. Yvonne, like many, saw The View and the press conference. So, Personnel knows where she was for the last ten years she prayed about the job, but she got nothing. Just before going to see Yvonne Stones, she said God I prayed about this, if you are answering, I can't hear you. So, she finds herself accepting her old job. She is to start in three weeks when Mrs. Lawrie goes on maternity leave. There is a possibility she will not return, wanting to stay home, or at least stay for two years with the twins. Martha feels a jolt. She feels as if her heart is being squeezed. From a distance she hears Mrs. Stones anxious voice asking if she is alright. She takes a deep breath and assures her she is alright, just gas or nerves. She forces a smile and asks how many of the old staff are still there. (Mrs. Lawrie, she knows is new). Mrs. Stone said they can walk down to the department to see. Suddenly, Martha feels shy and nervous. It is said judgment from your peers is harsh. Compassion comes from elsewhere. Is this why she is hesitant? What if they reject her? What if they do not want to work with her? What if they all resign and leave her. There are six dieticians plus the supervisor, head of the department.

As they approach the door, Martha wonders why the only sound she hears is her thumping heart. It is so loud. It obliterates everything else. Yvonne Stone is talking, but she has difficulty hearing or understanding what she is saying. Then she opens the door and there's an explosion.

"Surprise!" Voices chorused. "Welcome back." Martha is stunned. There is Liz, Mary. Doreen, Melody and Nancy, the supervisor. And she cried and cried and cried amid hugs and kisses. They missed me. The thought flashed in her head. They seem like they missed me, she mused. The awkwardness she envisioned never showed up, and she is very glad.

"You still look gorgeous," said Mary. "You always knew how to wear makeup. Look at you, Miss sophisticate! Made-up and face impeccable. Dress flawless and those gorgeous legs. You don't really need to wear stockings; those legs are perfect."

Martha is a little self-conscious but laughs and thanks her. Where is Maxwell? She asked of no one in particular. Max is off today. He has a daughter and is the original doting, Papa. He broke up with Julie, so he spends every opportunity with Kayla, and Kiana said Mary.

"Oh, well I guess I will see him soon enough. Thank you so much guys for the warm welcome. I was afraid to come but you were. Acceptance means a lot to me. I will have to rely on your directions until I get my head back in the game."

"Oh, no worries girl. Just like riding a bicycle. You will see," said Doreen smiling. "Anyway, I have rounds. Gonna see baby Jake. Not because I have to, but I want to He is the 18 months old with seemingly various food allergies. He is so sweet." With that, she heads through the door with a brisk walk.

"So, in three weeks you start," said Mary. "This is exciting. You will bring some new energy and pep to the unit. And might I add it is well overdue. You were always a fitness buff, and we all thought you would be swept off your feet and taken away to some exotic place."

As everyone laughs. Martha answered jokingly. "I thought of it, but here tell the Saudi Prince is taken, so is Prince Rainier."

"Did Prince Rainier remarry?" asked Doreen.

"Doesn't have to, Princess Grace is always with him. And that, my friends, is the worst rival; legacy remembrance of a ghost." Martha laughs.

Melody invites her to lunch so she can renew her acquaintance with the cafeteria ware but, she politely declines saying she'll forego the pleasure but would accept coffee.

"Sure thing," said Melody. "Meet Juan Valdez." As the others laugh, Martha is handed a mug that said #1.

"Welcome home!" said Melody. "I'm happy you are back. We will kill the fatted calf when the older brother Max comes in."

Martha laughs at the joke as did Mary. Everyone knows Melody alluded to the story of the prodigal son. Martha stifles a yawn which Doreen saw. She apologizes, stating due to nervousness about the interview she did not sleep well the night before. She leaves shortly. She wants to find a quiet place with her thoughts. With great effort, she walks timely to the exit after hugging each coworker.

Martha's chest hurt. It was so painful, she takes several long, deep breaths to steady herself. When she believes her breathing is almost normal, she heads to the subway. The train should not be crowded. She needs Nana's love and pampering. She reaches Westchester in the early afternoon. She hugs Nana and breathes a sigh of relief.

"Rough day?" Nana asked.

"Sort of," she said. "I was nervous, had ambivalent feelings. I let my imagination run wild so now I feel drained."

"How did the interview go? Did you get the job? When do you start?" Nana asked.

"Oh," Nana. "Don't you ever take breath?" Interview went well, I got the job, and I start in three weeks.

"Oh, right. That's my girl. They should be darned glad to get you too."

Marty laughed. "Slow down, Nana. I guess all that enthusiasm has nothing to do with me being your granddaughter, right Grandma?" she teased.

Nana is unrepentant. "Well, I am allowed. It's bad enough you want to live elsewhere rather than right here with me. A perfectly good bedroom, no invasion of privacy."

"Grandma, you know it would not work. You would sit up waiting for me to get home, even at the ripe old age of thirty-five. Anyway, I enrolled in Divinity studies. My soul needs rest and peace."

"When are you going to tell your mother about her grandchildren? Darling, the longer you wait, the harder it's going to be. Do it soon, pumpkin, you know I will gladly be there with you when you tell your parents. Think of me as the spoon of sugar that will make the medicine go down in a more delightful way," Nana quoted in the correctly.

Martha nods acknowledging what Nana said. Giving her life to Christ would not make issues miraculously disappear. The promise is to trust, believe and have faith. He will go through it with you. She asks God to give her the courage to confess to what she has done. She must be honest if her life is to have meaning and affect others in a positive way. She has lunch with Nana. All the while thinking of the inevitable meeting with her parents. Ah, deception, she muses. You are an ugly mistress; you sit and wait to entrap the weak and vulnerable. Her lips twist without humor. What the heck was she thinking back then? Why did she not think there would be a day of reckoning? Where did she think it would go? She shakes her head. She has to do it soon. She recalls the 23rd Psalm: Yea though I walk through the valley of the shadow of death, I will fear no evil, for thou art with me; and Psalm 121: Behold, he that keeps Israel does not slumber nor sleep. She will use these verses to see her through.

Once she leaves Grandma, she heads for WASP headquarters. She will call her mom and set up a meeting with her. She knows once the appointment is made; she will not renege. She picks up the phone and dials. Grandma is right, there is no good that comes from delaying the inevitable. After the usual greetings to her mom, she asked when she and Dad would be free this week. Her mother wants to know if it is an emergency.

"No, mom. It's just vital and, this week seems to be good as any," she said brightly. (But inwardly before I lose my nerves).

Her mother agrees to Thursday- left to confirm with her father. As she ends with mundane small talk, Walter Scotts' "Oh what tangled web we weave when first we practice to deceive," plays in her mind. She sneers with dislike at the quote, while acknowledging the truth of it. To take her mind off things, she calls Gabriel, her grandson. He's excited to hear her.

"Hey, Auntie Marty. Where are you? Are you coming to get me? Hold on," he said, and he makes it a video call.

"Slow down, Gabe. I am not coming to get you, just want to speak with my favorite godson. So, what's going on?"

Gabriel launches into a long tale about his computer games. He plays soccer online.

"Who is winning?"

"That's easy. Gabriel is winning Gabe. The score is 3- 1."

"I guess you are alone and playing solo. Don't you have homework. Is that finished?"

"Oh Auntie! Why do you have to spoil it. Homework! He said, laughing. I finished my homework, so I get to play. How about a game Auntie?"

" Gabriel honey. I have no clue what that is or how to play it," she laughs.

"I can teach you how. There's nothing to it. Next time you come over. I'll give you your first lesson. Then when you are skilled, we will have a match."

"Okay, Gabriel, whatever you say, but how about homework? I do not want your mom, even if it's my best friend yelling at me. She gives the heart sign. I missed you; you know that."

Alright guys, I'm pretty unforgettable, huh Auntie Em?

"Yes, my favorite."

"I guess that's why the girls in my class make eyes at me." And she opens her eyes at him; he puts up his hand palms up. "I swear I do not encourage them but see them pecs. I have Michael Jordans abs."

"You know, boy, you are something else."

"See Auntie, I want to look like Tom Brady but run like Walter Payton. Gotta study the greats, Jim Brown, Eric Dickerson, etcetera. Coach, let us watch old games to motivate us."

"I will not rain on your dream. It's going to be hard work to show you are not another pretty face. Talent is key. Hard work, dedication, discipline and good grades are essential. Now get to your homework."

"Oh, Auntie Em."

"Don't Auntie Em me. I really love you, not obsessed or bowled over by your looks. You are handsome, but education counts. Go- Git shaking her fist at him playfully. Later, baby love you."

"Love you too," Auntie, he says and hangs up.

She always feels good after talking with Gabriel. As she thinks about him, she remembers her Gabriel. He is a handsome lad. He seems pleasant, mannerly, if somewhat shy. She remembers how adorable he was as a baby. She had fallen so hopelessly in love with him, she had to cut loose. Now he has no idea who she is. She cannot take credit for his upbringing. She was not there for the first time when he fell off his bike or skinned his knee. She can't take credit for any of the external stuff. But she can take credit for giving birth to him. It is small comfort that he was stolen, and she did not give him up for adoption. She's positive DNA test would show he is hers, but she had her reasons back then and never pursued it.

As Martha says goodbye to Gabriel, she lies across the bed. She has to rehearse what she's going to say to her parents. Before long, it will be Thursday. She wonders if she should take the coward's way out and have Nana there for support. Yes, she decides she should. Then another thought enters her head. What if they get upset because she told Nana before them. Oh boy this is not going well. She abruptly sits up in bed. She reaches for her phone and googles Cece Winans, For the Goodness of God. No one sings it like CeCe. She listens a number of times and then Every Praise by Hezekiah Walker. Those songs are mood changers. She loves the video with the multi group singing and dancing in the road. As a matter of fact, she'll just listen to, two hours of Best Gospel music of all times. As she absorbs the music, she feels calm. Music does give you rest. She remembers a professor saying music can give even the savage rest. She continues to listen to the music. She does not want any interruption. It occurs to her she should tell her paternal grandparents, Wes and Gertrude Chimes. Now she would definitely meet at Nanas house, so she makes the call.

Chapter 2

Thursday starts out cloudy, then gives way to sunshine. Martha and Nana prepared oatmeal cookies, tea, coffee, lemonade, croissants and tostones with garlic butter dip. The house smells so good with the baked treats. There's no cohesiveness to the food prepared for the guests. It is to please the palate and maybe distract. Both parents and grandparents reached within moments of each other. Amid the hugs and kisses Martha directs them to the kitchen. It is big and cozy, complete with a breakfast nook with a banquet. The kettle and coffee pots are on the counter, while the food is on the dining table. Appreciative sniffs are heard, and Nana offers the treats.

"Oh my! this smell great and look heavenly but I can see the calories," said Gertrude.

"Come on, Gertrude, you have nothing to worry about. Wouldn't hurt to give Wes some meat to hold on to" said Nana outrageously, laughing heartily.

"No need to tell me twice. They beckon and they come. They call. And I answer," said Dad. There is general laughter.

"Yes, I can see. What do you mean Gerty? (Mom knows Grandma hates the shortening of her name), but like Mom says, give the man some meat to hold on to. You don't mind; do you honey?" She said with a mischievous look and he kissed her.

"Of course I don't mind. Think what fun it will be to take it off later and I will help you exercise."

While Grandpa guffaw much to the discomfort of his wife, Martha smiles and shakes her head. For a while she forgets the arduous task ahead of her. Grandma Gertrude accepts tea and croissants. With the almost jovial atmosphere, Martha's confidence lifts. Maybe food will mellow her audience when they finish drinking coffee and tea. Martha addressed the family.

She thanked them for coming. She has information to tell them, and she's asking that, she narrates her story without interruption. It's difficult for her, so she wants to finish once she starts. The questions can come after. However, at the end, she is hoping that each one will forgive her. Living a life for Christ, she has to be honest with her family. And she begins her narrative.

When she dated Ogwin she got pregnant. When she found out, she was afraid to tell her parents. She debated what to do, and when she told Ogwin, he said he did not want to be a father, wanted to pursue his career and had no time to be a father. She graduated and because she was enrolled in the bachelor's program at Brooklyn College, didn't worry too much about college. Ogwin decided she should terminate her pregnancy. He found a doctor who turned out to be a quack who botched the termination. He was a doctor from the East who was incompetent. She started bleeding and he said something went wrong. By some miracle the pregnancy didn't end. She went to Bristol Street Clinic in East New York for privacy, to prevent running into someone she knew. After she was examined by the nurse practitioner, she left Bristol Street Clinic and headed to Manhattan. She went to Central Park and met a couple, Rebecca and Stan, who explained their long journey to have a child. At that point, she decided she'd put the baby up for adoption.

She did not want to raise a baby by herself. She was afraid, really terrified. She felt guilty and like a hypocrite. She remembered how she lied to mom that she was a virgin and not having sex with Ogwin when she realized how hurt her mother and father would be, she decided she'd leave home. I imagined and believed the worst that she would never be forgiven. She thought of the embarrassment her parents would face. She thought of Denise, Yvonne, and Calvin how disappointed they'd be. She knew Grandma Gertrude would find a way to blame Mom. I cried for several days and nights but, was too cowardly to tell anyone. Not even the Brooklyn Divas knew, she could not trust anyone. She berated herself for her stupidity. She thought to ask Nana for help, but she wanted it to be a secret. She didn't want to put Nana in that position to lie to her daughter and possibly cause a rift in the family. Then she had found that Catholic Charities had a program for teenage mothers. It seemed ideal, she could have anonymity. She got an identification which gave me a new name and birthday. So, I went to Mount Vernon, where she checked in Sisters of Mercy Home for Unwed Mothers. She stayed until she gave birth and her daughter was put up for adoption. By this, her mother was sobbing with her father holding her. She ignored the sobs and the occasional gasp from Grandma Gertrude.

She had to continue. Now it was a monologue. There was a doctor who took care of the girls there. She shared house with seven other girls run by Sister Catherine and Sister Petrona and Sister Grace. They were kind. The girls and I became friends. My roommate was Sasha. She was 18 years. Her boyfriend forgot he slept with her, which put her scholarship to Syracuse in jeopardy. Not all the girls put their children up for adoption. Others kept their babies and stayed. But others went back to school. When I went to Bristol clinic, the NP said she noticed scarring and if I had attempted to terminate the pregnancy and I ran from that clinic, not wanting to hear more. What if the baby was deformed? Since I had no prenatal care until I went to Mount Vernon, the doctor, Gruniche did not mention anything about the attempted abortion. What he didn't say either was that I was carrying twins. It was a difficult delivery; blood pressure dropped, went in and out of consciousness. But I remember I saw my daughter and later I woke up and saw a second baby that was whisked away by the doctor and his nurse. Later he tried to convince me there was no second child, then later that the baby was stillborn. I know I heard the baby cry, and it was a little boy. Don't ask me how I knew it was a boy. I told him still born baby couldn't cry. He took me to see a stillborn baby in the hospital morgue. Deep in my heart I knew he was alive. I found out the doctor stole my baby. He had an adoption agency and his kindness to the Sisters of Mercy was to have access to unwed mothers and to find 'good' homes for them. However, my friends and I tracked him to Westchester. And I took pictures of him under the guise of looking for a part time job for when I started college. I went to Connecticut, but they lived in Westchester but had a landscaping business in Connecticut. Talking with the owner, he proudly showed a picture of a newborn. He was proud of my Gabriel. I named him that. I was shocked and when he asked if I was okay told I had not eaten, but his son looked exactly like my brother. They could pass for twins. So, that's how I saw him properly for the first time. Meanwhile, the family that got my daughter by arrangement agreed to name her Sarai as a middle name and I gave them a bracelet for her. Without that agreement, I would have stopped adoption. If I had not run from the Bristol clinic, maybe I would have known I was carrying twins. I would never have given up my daughter for adoption. I would never separate the twins, and I would've come home. The doctor never told me he and his nurse were bartering babies. When I made a stink, he set the office on fire, burning all the records, leaving his nurse to face the music. He moved to Venezuela. I do not know where my daughter is, but I know where my Gabriel is. He is here in Westchester. I saw him when I was first paroled. I know what a mess I got myself in because of pride, stupidity, arrogance. I should not be in such a position. I didn't want anyone to know my shame, but for all my academic prowess, I fell victim to being a statistic. I was afraid I wouldn't be able to cope with being a parent on my own. All I could do was keep in touch by phone. I missed you all so much. I believe separation was just payment for my sins; that I deserved the loneliness, and the self-recriminations. I was suffering, but I felt revived when I called and heard your voices, though I said nothing at the other end. I just believed I did not deserve to have a family.

Her mother was bawling. Both grandmothers were sobbing.

"Please forgive me, Mom and dad," she pleaded. "I am so very, very, sorry. I wish I could go back and change this outcome. I'd throw myself at your mercy. It's been too hard. And now she was sobbing and down on her knees in front of her parents, pleading and begging for forgiveness.

"Oh Martha, Martha, you are my daughter. Why couldn't you come to me?" said her mother.

"Alright." Dad comforted my mother. Silent tears ran down his cheeks. Grandpa was holding grandma and Nana picked me up and hugged me.

"Hush child, hush. You have suffered enough. This is too much burden for one person to shoulder. It's over now, it's not a secret anymore, and it's about time. Forgive yourself," Nana said softly.

Her mother and father looked shocked, baffled, confused and stupefied. Martha could feel genuine compassion for them. It is bad enough she was 'a runaway' but omitted to tell them she was pregnant and gave birth! Whether they decided to forgive her or not, she could harbor no ill feeling towards them. She loved them and would always love them; likewise, her grandparents.

"This is awful, so awful. I am stunned. "Oh dear," said Grandma Gertrude clutching her chest. I do not know how I'm going to hold my head up. The embarrassment and shame of it!" and she started sobbing.

"Now, dear, do not upset yourself so. She was young, and maybe she should have told us before, and maybe we would have got that young cad to marry her. And maybe this is not our brightest hour, but we are not going to tell anyone. Most families have a skeleton or two in the closet. Dry your eyes," and hands her a handkerchief.

"Marty, my dear, I am so sorry that our stance made it such you felt you could not trust us to understand or forgive. I am not happy, but I cannot blame you. You were but a child and making adult decisions." After kissing his wife, walked over to Marty hugs and kisses her on the forehead. She feels comfort as his arms close around. She exhales deep cleansing breaths.

Through sniffles her mother mumbles, "Wesley is right. You were a child. I am sorry for your ordeal. I am hurt, I won't lie, but I am sorrowful because you hurt. I would have preferred my daughter with a baby than the long lonely years without you." She holds out her hands. "Please excuse me, I have to talk to my daughter alone."

As her father turns to accompany them. Her mom says, "No Cliff," turns and kisses his cheek.

Marty hugs her father, apologizing again with her eyes. He squeezes her, kissing the top of her head. They walk to the bedroom. Once inside her mom closes the door, directs her to sit.

"Good Lord Martha was I such an ogre you couldn't talk to me? Yes, I would've been angry but to go through a pregnancy alone? Dear Marty, I love you. I would've gotten over it in time. Now I have two grandchildren I will never meet. Where are the pictures of the boy."

Martha smiles through tear filled eyes and shows her Peter James Dunstan; the three she got as a baby and later two at age two. She feels an overwhelming love for her two children. Her mother gawks at the pictures. Fresh tears cruise her cheeks.

"So precious, so precious. You say you saw him once since you came home?"

"Yes mother. I saw him by the park one day playing with friends. I talked with him, and he was polite. I was so happy to see him. Athletic built, smooth mahogany skin free from blemish, he's really handsome."

"Take me to the park. I want to see my grandson."

"Not so easy mom. He would be at school now. Maybe on a Saturday we could go and see if he is there," Martha said quietly.

Disappointment is etched in her mother's face, then she shakes her head. She hugs her mother.

"I don't know what to do," her mother wailed.

"There is nothing to do, Martha said sympathetically. I never tried to get Gabriel aka Peter back. I know he was stolen from me but, if I had known I was carrying twins I would never consider adoption. Dr. Gruniche is a piece a turd, a slimy little man, a snake. For years I hoped he was rotting in a Venezuelan jail or covered with sores all over for what he did. I repented for those thoughts. I am or learning forgiveness mom. I have to forgive. Christ died for me for the mess I've made. And he forgave me for hurting you, Dad, my siblings and my grandparents. So, I have to forgive him."

"Okay darling but we must find your daughter."

"Mom, I signed the papers without coercion. I agreed to it."

"Yes. But you were underage. No court declared you an independent minor. Martha, that decision was made because the doctor withheld vital information from you. You said if you knew you were carrying twins, there would never have been an adoption; Isn't that, right?"

"Yes, mom but, there is something else."

"And what is that?"

"Well, when I gave birth, it wasn't as Martha Chimes but Novelette Masters."

"What? Come again. Repeat please! You did what? I always thought tv was a corrupt influence making it seem like parents were figure heads. I was right. What you think your life is a soap opera. Oh Lord. Oh, my Lord." And then she starts to laugh then to cry. Mom is hysterical.

"Oh, Mom please!" She pushes her in the armchair and hugs her. Don't cry Mom. I am so, sorry. I am so, so sorry. I wish I could change the past. But I can't have a do over. I never saw the future, just the present. All I knew to do then was survive. In hindsight it was stupid and selfish."

By this her father burst into the room.

"What in tarnation is going on?" He asked looking from mother to daughter. "Well," he prompted as he closes the door.

"I don't know Cliff. Your daughter, your daughter...."

It was a familiar scene. Whenever her mother was mad at her she was Cliff's daughter.

"What has my daughter done?" he asked.

"Hasn't she done enough. Hasn't she?"

"Yes, honey, but what additional sin has she committed? You are hysterical, darling," he said soothingly while pulling her in his arms and rubbing her back.

If the situation wasn't so dire she would've found the situation amusing. What is the saying, the more things change the more they remain the same. Her mother raves and cries and her father soothe and calms. And just for a minute Martha was transported home again with them, and it was good. And she cried again for lost childhood and the familial ritual that was theirs. She repeated the birth dilemma to her dad.

"Any more surprises Marty. I am getting old. Tell me now. Anything you want to say about your incarceration?"

"No, Dad. I was exonerated, you know that. I sin against God and you with having children outside marriage. Yes, I did the unpardonable. I did not trust my parents. I did not want my actions to reflect on you. So that's why I worked at distancing myself from the family. Guilt is a burden that it's the heaviest load a man or woman can ever carry. It shrinks you, robs you of sleep, purpose, perception and rationale, and that's why it drives some people crazy, literally," she said feelingly.

"Okay, baby. I am not blaming you. I know you suffered. It is in your eyes. Why make you feel any worse than you do? You've beaten yourself up enough." He is rocking his wife while talking.

She envies the love they share, even after all these years. Her dad is still so handsome, a good six feet and mom 5-6, still pretty and in her prime. Mom, Dad, she whispered inwardly. I love you both so much. My delinquency is not a reflection of you. Hope you will forgive me completely one day. Nana, always the hostess, has fresh coffee and tea she offers to cook. She offered to cook her special turkey meatballs with brown rice and peas, stirred fried vegetables and pork chops in gravy. Her paternal grandmother declines, and Nana got her skillet to do her version of pan-seared chops. Dorette offers to help and Nana shoos her daughter and son-in-law to go rest on the futon. Martha kisses Nana.

"What is that for?"

"Thank you, Nana, you are a pillar of strength. Thank you for always being in my corner."

"No need child. You are like my very own. Plus, that's any respectable grandmother's job. It wasn't as bad as I think, it could have been worse with your Park Slope Brooklyn socialite grandparents," Nana said, laughing. "See my Harry. God rest his soul. Not a pretentious bone in his body. Wonderful man! Gone to quick. Best husband ever next to your dad. Gladly own him as a son-in-law several times over."

They bustle in the kitchen with dinner preparations working harmoniously. Much later, her grandmother asks, "So, what was the caterwauling about."

"I told Mom that I used an alias when I gave birth. I guess it tipped her over the edge. Martha Chimes did not give birth but Novelette Masters. She was ready to go look for her grandchildren, you see, so now she can't."te

"Poor Dorette. Did you tell her the grandson lives nearby?"

"Yes, Nana, I did. Stop scowling grandma, she has a right to. I messed up big time. I kept in touch with you, sort of, but not with her. Grandma, that's rejection by any standard. And for a proud Mama a slap in the face. You've had a while to process this and forgive me. Poor mom, so disappointed. And who can blame her?"

"I don't blame her for feeling disappointed or hurt. She will get over it. She has a loving husband. Who will convince her your misdeeds has nothing to do with her."

"Do you know Nana for years I broke into cold sweat when I thought I almost aborted two babies. I could have lost my life because of that quack."

"Well, Marty they say man appoints and God disappoints. I'm sure glad He did."

"You know, I went all out to find Gabriel aka Peter. And people might think it's strange that I signed the adoption paper for his sister so why track him down? But I heard Gabriel's cry. And it was like he was calling out to me. I was in a fog but that plaintive cry touched me deep down. You know, like he was telling me I am here, wanting me to take him. Doctor Gruniche tried to convince me I was mistaken, but that baby tugged at my heart. I was so ecstatic when I found Jonathan and Esther Dunston. And the best part? they lived in Westchester. I got to be with him. He was a delightful baby. So many times, I was tempted to take him, but I knew they'd hunt me down and there'd be a scandal. And that's when I separated from him. It was getting harder and harder to see him. I loved him so much. There is some comfort that I know what he looks like and where he is. We will go Saturday to the park and see if we see him," she promised.

"Did you tell your Mama that?"

"No, I did not get that far. I will though Grandma, I would love to see my daughter Sarai. I gave the mother a bracelet for her with a heart inscribed, mother's pride'. Without the condition the adoption was off also I must meet the parents, even though we wore masks. I must see their eyes and have verbal assurance to cherish Sarai. The baby's middle name must be Sarai. The conditions were met, I believe, as a priest was there. It was a different kind of adoption. Even then Nana I had reservations and doubt. I should have just called you," she said.

"Water under the bridge, Ducky. Water under the bridge. I wish with all my heart to meet my great grandchildren. Your sister doesn't seem to be in a hurry to have any. What's she waiting on?"

"Oh, Nana. Many career women start their family after they are somewhat established and in their thirties. I heard this lady say people behave as if it was a crime she didn't have a child in her early twenties. She has one now and she's sure the same amount of trouble she gives now is the same she would have back then, so what's the rush? She didn't miss anything."

Nana laughs. "You know pumpkin, she's right. You know what that reminds me of. Hear tell that this man lived with this woman. They had maybe six-seven children, so when the first child turned 25 the lady said to him, Bailey, I think we should get married. The children are big and are adults now. Don't you think it's time we got married. Uh-huh, he said. What's the rush? You're going somewhere."

Both laughed at the tale. Nana checks the red peas, they are soft, and she adds coconut milk, garlic, scallion, thyme, and pepper. As the seasonings blend, the aroma tantalizes the nose and heightens the senses. Martha loves that scent. When I grow up, I want to be a terrific cook like Nana, she says to herself. Within the hour, dinner is ready. Before they sit to eat, they say grace blessing the food- for the provision. Martha made sure to be standing next to her mother so they could hold hands. Her eyes reflect her feelings. The rice and peas, the pork chops and turkey meatballs are beyond delicious. The chops are sitting on the rice, escorted by the meatballs, flanked by lettuce and tomatoes is a sight. Martha snaps a picture to tantalize members of WASP, especially Bethanne and Keisha. A mischievous smile plagues her lips as she sends it to them. She will be careful not to look at her phone; better she turns it off.

Dinner is a little awkward at first but her father compliments Nana on being a great cook.

"So, what about me?' Her mother asked.

"Of course you are my lovely. Can't you tell you inherited that gift?" he said, kissing her cheek.

Martha smiles. Her mother is a reasonably good cook. She makes a mean chicken soup, fried chicken, macaroni and cheese and short ribs. Martha eats with restraint, which Nana noticed.

"Why, Marty, are you picking at your food?"

"I'm doing well Nana, I have enough to eat."

"You are not modeling anymore. And nothing is wrong with having some meat on those bones."

Martha laughs. "All true, Grandma. But you know what they say. From the lips straight to the hips."

There is general laughter. Her father ever mischievously looks at his wife.

"Is that right, honey? Stand let me see you. Guess you are right, Marty."

His wife jobs him in annoyance.

"See, he says to no one in particular; Spousal abuse- that's what this is."

"And I guess you are sleeping out tonight," her mother said sweetly.

"No. I am going home. Mom, do you see her threatening me, trying to put me out of the matrimonial bed," her father said.

"Dorrette play nice! Kiss and makeup or I'll send you to your room."

"You know, Mother, for once I'd love it if you take up for me. You swapped me the day I introduced Cliff to you. Why don't you ever take up for me?"

"Play nice," said Grandma. "Kiss and makeup; now Dorrett."

Martha can see her father enjoying this. Nana loves him and never hesitates to show him preference. Her father puckered up, eyes closed for the kiss and her mother leans forward and at the last second kissed him on the cheek. They all laugh while her mother looks smug. The old camaraderie is back. Her parents used to always behave like this. Nana invariably sides with her son-in-law and mother always fuss. 'She forgets I am her daughter.' Grandpa Bob would kiss her cheeks. Martha missed that. What did that say? If I could only turn back the hands of time. She sighs inwardly so true. Everything is pleasant, but there is an elephant in the room as the dishes are cleared away and tea and coffee are served. Martha turns on her phone, relishing the annoyance of her friends. She is smiling as she washes the dishes.

"Leave those Marty, I will get them later. Come sit with us."

"No Nana, I am almost done anyway. I'll be there in a jiffy."

Martha packages food for her parents. Nana always cooks as if she's feeding an army. There is so much food. She decides to visit WASP tomorrow and bring some. Nana won't mind. She loves to cook and is always feeding people. As a child she remembered being sent to Miss Rose with a plate, to Mr. Clark, Mr. Parks, Miss Glenda, and many more. God bless her giving heart, she said inwardly. She joins them in the living room.

"No desserts?" she asked.

"My hips can't afford it. said her mother. As her father opens his mouth her mother said, "Shush Cliff! Not a word."

"Mum is the word," he said smiling. He is unrepentant.

Martha and Nana exchange looks. "It is so gratifying to have my most favorite persons visiting. This old heart is very glad. This is the very best gift. And so now we are full. We can plan. Marty has something to share with you.

"I do?" said Martha stupefied.

"Yes, Marty. Tell them about Gabriel."

"What Nana? Oh, I plan to go to the park this Saturday to see if I see him. I believe he will talk with me. I believe he feels a connection between us. I will tell him I used to babysit him." And said inwardly what I won't tell him is that I breast fed him; that I did it numerous times. That is my secret. When Esther wondered why he loved her so much she never let on, she was bonding with her child. After all, he was stolen from her. She remembered the reverence of it all, the intimacy of that mother and child moment as he fed and she nurtured. It was great revenge when he rejected her/Esther breast feeding him. One day, maybe when he's an adult, she'll tell him. She now knows that King David has it right. Psalm 127:3-5 Behold children are a heritage from the Lord, the fruit of the womb a reward. However, verse 3 resonates with her, so she memorized it.

"Marty, Marty! Are you in there?" her grandmother said.

She jumps. She was miles away. "Sorry I was back in the past, but I'm here now. What did you say?"

"Dor wants to come to on Saturday."

"Sure, Mom. But it cannot seem as if we ambush him. We have to plan. What to do and the approach is critical. "We don't want to spook him," said Martha.

They plan to have a picnic nearby where he was playing the last time. It will be a family having fun. Martha will seek him out and offer him and his friends' water if necessary. They will get to the park at about 11:00-ish complete with blankets, Bose Music, scrabble cards and Domino's. They are 'going' country minus the plaid shirts and polyester bell bottoms with suspenders. No need to frighten the neighborhood. As planned, her parents reached Nana's home and they packed water, sandwiches, jerk chicken, fruits and games and head for the park. There are children there along with adults. Just as long as it doesn't get crowded Martha welcomes the adults, so they do not appear conspicuous.

Soon a group of boys came with footballs. They seem to pick teams. Each team has four members. After much bickering, they started playing four on four football. Well, at least they are inventive. There is also a make-believe end zone. Martha spots Gabriel aka Peter. They play for a while and one of the team scores a touchdown. His teammates yelled, "That's glorious," and starts to dance. They play for almost an hour. Then they came to rest.

Martha saunters over and greets the boys. "So, who is Eli Manning, and the T Brady, Peyton Manning, Aaron Rodgers. I just witnessed the pass and touch down, said Martha.

"Hi, ma'am," they said.

"Good game, but you didn't answer. Who is Eli Manning and Tom Brady."

They laugh, one lad said, we are not really good, we just like the game. We are just 'wanna bes'. The others laugh.

"You a football fan?" asks the smallest in the group.

"Yes and no. I just get excited near Super Bowl time. Yes, I get the fever like most persons just before the final four," Martha said smiling.

Peter is looking at her, head one side. "I remember you. I saw you about three months ago right here."

"That is true. I said hello to you."

"Yeah, I wondered why. Do you know me because I don't know remember but, you seem familiar. Are you someone famous?"

"I know you. I used to babysit you when you were a baby up to about two years old. I was in college then, but I remember you."

"Wow! Are you kidding me. My babysitter; that's incredible!"

"Sure, you can tell your mom Esther and dad Johnathan, you saw Martha and she said hello." She pulls her ID and shows him.

"Now I know where I saw you. You were o tv. You were charged with murder, but DNA proved you didn't," said Peter.

"You remember well," said Martha.

"Hey guys, this is Martha. She used to babysit me. This is Troy, Maurice, Kenrick, Ron and Scott."

"Hi Martha," they said.'

"Can you tell us what he was like. Anything bad that we can use," asked Troy.

"Fraid not. He was the cutest, most loving baby. I loved caring for him, but he could run and loved to eat," she said.

"Well, this boy has a big appetite. He is banned from (all the) all-you-can-eat buffets. That's why they all closed," said Scott.

"Do you all go to the same high school?"

"Yes. We go to Lefferts High," Ron said. "Did you go there too?"

"I went to Midwood High School. I'm a Brooklynite. Nana lives here. We used to come for vacation, Easter, summer and Christmas. Nana is a lot of fun. The lady in the blue top and slacks is Nana, my grandmother, and that's my mom and dad."

"I am thirsty," piped Scott.

"Oh, I can give you a bottle of water if you like."

"Yes, thank you."

"Anyone else, Peter?" said Martha.

"How is it you ask Peter by name," said Troy. "And I am much cuter than him. Handsome, really."

The others laugh.

"He's always like that. Must be the center of attention," someone said.

The boys walk towards Martha as she leads them towards her family. She takes the water from the igloo and hands to each boy. She introduces the boys. "Peter here, I used to babysit while I was in college."

Her mother's eyes popped open wide. Then she shutters them. They greet the boys and offer food as well, but they decline. The boy's trot off to continue their game. As the boys are out of ear shot, her mother said.

"Oh Marty, he is a fine boy. Oh, I would love to hug him and hold him. This cannot be right." And she started to cry. Her father moves to comfort her. Martha walks away. Everything she does seems to be a mistake. 'God, where are you? Why can't I feel you? Lord, make haste to rescue me. Isn't that what Psalm 70 verse one says? She remembers Reverend Arthur Caliendo of Marble Collegiate Church always used to say it. She can't ask him now. She has the urge to be alone. Lo and behold her son that she can't claim! She was not prepared for the wrenching pain at actually touching him. And when he smooched her cheek, she died. And she cried inside. Will she have this pain continuously? She folds her hands around her middle to stop the pain. She is short of breath. From a distance it seems a voice is calling her.

"Marty. Marty, wake up."

She came to with three anxious tear-filled faces hovering above her. Now what is going on? She wondered, briefly closing her eyes.

"Martha. Martha."

"Yes, Mom. What is the matter?"

"One minute you are standing and the next you are crumpled to the ground. Luckily, it's all grass, said Nana. Easy baby," as Martha tries to sit up.

"I don't know why I fainted. I've never fainted in all my life," she said. (Then inwardly it's been a very traumatic week; fear, stress, guilt, remorse, regret all intertwine).

"Pumpkin. Do you think you need to talk to someone? All this is too much. I am sorry I added to your burden. I can see now you are not ready for that maelstrom of emotions, close proximity to your son invokes," said her mother.

"It's the ambivalence that is the creature. How can I hurt the Dunstons? What if Peter/ Gabriel hates me? What if he resents my not identifying who I was years ago and worked to get him back? Am I strong enough to withstand that kind of rejection? I can't seem to hear God. I'm praying but it does not seem as if He is anywhere near me."

"Hush, child. God is ever near. He will never leave you nor forsake you; in his own time, for, he that keeps Israel neither slumber nor sleep. Psalm 27 verse 14 says; Wait on the Lord. Be of good courage, and he shall strengthen thine heart. Wait, I say, on the Lord." Nana quoted.

Her fainting put a somber mood on the picnickers. They got what they came for, but was it worth it? Martha reasoned that the three most important family members got to meet her son. Whether it resolves anything, she doesn't know. Now she is not obligated to take this any further. They or each of them can come to the park to see him. He seems an intelligent kid and will remember them. She is aroused from her reverie.

"Honey child, remember. You have already been forgiven. You are forgiven. The evil one wants to let you relive and rehash what has already been settled. Remember, he is the accuser of the brethren. Anytime the devil says guilty; say Jesus paid it. Whatever happens, will, in due course. You pray and agonize enough. Leave it with Jesus. That's a burden. Cast your burden on him. Give it to him, baby, all of it. Family, let us pray," said Nana.

And Nana prayed from Psalm 121 and Psalm 23. Lifting up eyes to the hills from whence comes help to lead me beside still waters to restore the soul. After the prayer, she sang:

"All your anxiety, all your care, take it to Jesus and leave it there. Never a burden he cannot bear. Never a friend like Jesus."

With normalcy returning. They played Scrabble. Martha and her dad are avid players. She remembered one time they played until past midnight as no one would give in. He had told her she inherited the scrabble gene. It got to the point they were spelling to, and the. They played until after three and left the park. They never saw Peter and his friends after that. The park got crowded, so they could have slipped by unnoticed. Martha was thankful for Nana. She has the ability to make quick assessments of needs. When Nana prays, it's like a ceremony. Martha said to herself she knows how to pray. When I grow up, I want to pray like her. Much later that night, she noticed a message on her phone. Her heart contracted. Nothing is going to upset her tonight. Tomorrow is soon enough. She picks up her Bible and reads Psalm 70, 121 and 23. Bless you King David, you cover everything. What if she could write like David would she have joy and peace. David was not perfect. He committed adultery and murder. He repented and moved on.(Psalm 51). It is said David is a man after God's heart, so there is hope for her. She heard a televangelist say before Christ came to earth and died, we under the law, we would pay for our sins, but Christ paid the price so we are no longer under the law. The upcoming week, she will have more questions for her divinity teachers.

After church on Sunday, she calls Judge Earl's mother, Nora. Nora congratulates her for her release and reversal of conviction. She wants Martha to visit her. Martha is not in a rush to meet her. She suddenly feels afraid. She is baffled by the uneasiness she feels having met Nora ten years ago. She was affable then. What if Nora believes she is guilty? And the civility now is just a front because she is acquitted of that murder. She remembered the interview on The View. Maybe Nora saw it. She tries to put Nora off. She has to study for finals and has papers due that she needs to complete and hand in. In the end, she tells Nora she'll try to rearrange her schedule for Saturday and let her know. Thankfully, she has term papers to hand in and finals to study for. She is meeting WASP on Saturday; she will let Keisha track her and listen in.

For devotion that morning, she reads Psalm 23 and 91. She needs to be fortified, she asks Nana to pray for her. As Martha walks from the subway at East. 96th St. she recited Psalm 23, verse 4- 5.

Yeah, though I walk through the valley of the shadow of death, I will fear no evil, for thou art with me. Thy rod and thy staff, they comfort me.

She finds 309 E 94th St. as she nears the building she. I'm looking up here. She cuts across the schoolyard where children are playing. Some are on slides, jungle gym, and shooting hoops. Some of the young men playing hoops call to her, but she waves and hurries through the gate. It is remarkable how some people can identify people who do not live in the neighborhood. That must be a talent, she mused. Now Apt B10. where are you? She scans the bells and finds it eventually.

"Okay Keisha, I've reached." As she turned around to walk towards the elevator a slim man enters the lobby. He says hello and goes to the left. She heads to the elevator but as the door closes sees the man. She is disappointed he gets in the elevator.

"You are visiting?" he asked. She nods.

"I know I would certainly have noticed someone like you." She smiles and still doesn't answer.

"I can see you are not very talkative, miss?"

She gives him the look, like really, but he is not deterred. When did four flights become so long? He holds out his hand. It is a well-manicured hand. Her eyes travel up to his face. A touch of gray at the temples, smooth teak color and beard nicely trimmed. Quite a pleasing picture!

"Now you have looked me over, am I pleasing to the Fair Lady?" He asked pleasantly.

She smiles in exasperation. "My mother says not to speak to strangers," she said.

He stares at her; the white even teeth and dimples caught his attention. He is truly captivated now." We can remedy that now. My name is Antonio Range Wilder," he said, stretching his hand forth. She shakes his hand." Martha Renee."

"No last name. Here's my business card. Brick and Woodward investment. Inc., She takes it and thanks him.

"Oh, just one minute. As she gets ready to step off the elevator. He flips his billfold and shows his driver's license. This is for your purpose that I am who I say I am. You intrigue me, Martha Renee. So, you are on your way to see Dowager Frontes."

"How do you know that?" she asked.

"See, there's a mirror in the elevator that gives a reflection. I know she lives at D10. I saw it." "Very observant of you, Mr. er. Wilder. Sure, you're not CIA? Have a great rest of your day."

"And you as well. However, if you need a ride, please call the cell phone."

"Thank you, but I am sure I don't need it but, thanks again."

To her surprise, he steps partially off, pointing towards Apt 10. As she raises her hand to ring the bell, he steps back into the elevator. She subconsciously listens for the elevator to move but she does not hear it. Her listening stops as the door swings open and Earle's sister Isabelle is there, perfectly manicured, hair in place. With red lipstick and form fitting dress, Martha greets her without shaking hands. She realizes she has reason to be concerned. This feels like an ambush. Girl is dressed to the 9th with heels! She is led in a foyer and through a small sitting room. This is a very nice apartment, so spacious. Martha notices the furniture in French provincial style. Martha knows it's a blend of French countryside with Parisian elegance. She admires the carved moldings and ornate work. The sofas are in muted shades of peach, ivory with splashes of lilac and mint. Isabelle is watching her through slits, yes black as coal.

"Mother, your guest is here," said Isabelle.

She moves to the doorway. Martha is standing, looking around casually. She is not offered a seat, so she'll wait for the Dowager elder Frontes. Before long, she flows in on a cloud of perfume, hair piled high, tall and elegant.

"Oh, Miss Chimes, her hands reach out to Martha. Isabelle, where's your manners? You did not offer a chair. Thank you so much for coming. I wanted to see you for the last time before I retreat to our estate in Connecticut. I'm old now and want to retire in peace. But I felt it made sense to do this now."

"That is kind of you Mrs. Frontes but wholly unnecessary. You gave me a gift ten years ago by believing I was innocent. As a mother, I know how hard that must have been. It helped a great deal. You cannot imagine how powerful that is."

"Thank you my dear for saying so. However, people change. Sometimes people are forced to make decisions they would not do ordinarily."

"My only concern is getting back to being free and not controlled by a clock or guards; when you can eat, shower, or go out in the fresh air. You have to be deprived of those simple things to appreciate all we take for granted. I need to work, and I have to finish Seminary; I'm completing a Master of Divinity. I learned the hard way in prison. There's nothing glamorous about being locked away for ten years. I cannot imagine what you are talking about. What decision is that?"

"I called you here to keep my Earle's memory intact. I know I have no right to ask, but an old woman has her pride. I was prepared to do anything to maintain his secret shame and mine as well. I've lived on pins and needles once I realized I admitted to you; I knew of my son's misdeed. I have lived with the possibility you would reveal it, so today I would offer you anything by fair means or force."

"Mrs. Frontes, you have nothing to fear from me. I could have offered that information at trial but didn't. You forget how I felt about the judge. I might have been repulsed by his fondness for young girls, but I felt drawn to him; I was attracted to him. I pleaded for his life. I put myself in harm's way for him. I still have the scar. I believed back then that maybe I could turn him from the sickness, because that's what it is. There was no finer man to look at. He was perfect in every way."

Marta turns her head and sees Isabelle drop two white tablets in a glass. Well, Isabella, Bella whatever name you use, we will share whatever you put in that class. She closes her eyes, afraid of what they may see.

"That is true," said Mrs. Frontes. You had the time and opportunity to reveal, but maybe you are not at the desperate stage yet. Oh, if only I could be sure."

"The fact that I have said nothing in ten years must count for something, I give you my word. It stays with me and you are making me uncomfortable. I will take my leave. Enjoy your retirement," she said.

She got up to leave and Bella says, "Well, umm with that assurance, let us toast to bury the past."

"Oh Isabella, did you not hear me tell your mom I am in seminary to get a master's in divinity? Therefore, alcohol is not a part of my life anymore, but you can go ahead."

"No, we should all do it," insisted Bella.

Martha asked that water be added to her drink to dilute its potency. Oh goodness she's looking for something to pour it in. Well, Coach Sofa, we are going to share today. With the planning in our head, she takes a delicate sip. "What is it anyway? asked Martha?"

"It is cream sherry; very mild and pleasant tasting," said Bella.

Martha turns to her sitting position and cradles the glass. She appears to take another sip and notices the look that passes between mother and daughter. Martha, grateful for the cloth sofa, pours half in the corner. Here in the bottom may be more potent than the top? She slashes its cherry on her arm in a jerky movement.

"Oh! I'm sorry I'm making a mess." She apologized. She uses a paper napkin to pat the wet area. Bella goes to the kitchen to get a towel. And her mouth tightened with annoyance while Nora clicks her tongue in gracious frustration.

"My dear, you have soiled your clothes."

"It's okay. Do not worry about it," said Martha.

"No, no, dear, wait. Can't, have you? smelling of liquor. I have a little spray that will remove the stain. I'll get it." said Nora.

Martha tiptoed and heard the two talking. She hears Nora say she's not sure any more about their plan. Maybe she's telling the truth. The drink spilling may be an indication it's over?

"Are you getting cold feet, mother? That is a small dose of BBR-barbiturate will not harm her, it will just reveal if she is hiding anything", said Bella.

"But what is the point now if she has? said nothing. Can we predict ten, fifteen years from now. Oh, my daughter, we did wrong."

"No mother. We go ahead; go to your room. I will question her. I believe she drank enough, "said Bella.

Martha returns to her seat and feigns sleepiness. She struggles to sit up as the pair enters.

"I believe I will leave soon. Because she stifles a yawn. I am feeling sleepy."

"Oh, so soon, said Bella. I would like to hear of your experience in jail, a sort of first scoop before you write your book," she said coaxingly.

"Write book? I am not writing a book. There's nothing glamorous about being in jail. That's something I want to put behind me. It matters I wasn't guilty. That is ten years I cannot get back. Do you think anything at all can compensate for being incarcerated? A bunch of quacks who conspired to have me convicted for a crime I didn't commit and the even bigger quack who was my lawyer, and I'm to glamorize that experience? You've got to be kidding."

"But didn't you dream of writing a tell all book you know? You were innocent, right? Isn't that something to look forward to?" persisted Isabelle.

"I can see you do not understand. Did you graduate college, Isabelle? And what, what college did you go? Let me break this down for you, because you really don't understand. I was not a nobody but a graduate student; a Registered Dietician. No one can compensate me for the hell I went through in jail. The only solace I had was the Bible. I watched some televangelists. I gravitated towards Billy Graham because that's who my grandmother loved. I watched Joel Osteen and Mr. Stanley. Listening to them gave me peace. Yes, I listened to TD Jakes and Fred Price. I had to saturate my soul. I was in a morass. And I needed to feel clean. I had to bury the attraction I felt for the judge and bury self. And I started to meditate on God's Word. The Bible became my companion. See. She opens her pocketbook and pulls out a tattered New Testament. This goes everywhere with me, the song says. Turn your eyes upon Jesus and things of earth will pale in significance to Jesus' light, glory and grace. As long as I read and listen to His words, I am good. The thief on the cross God redeemed him because he asked Jesus to remember him and he did," Martha said.

"I did not expect a sermon," said Isabelle.

"Well, what did you expect? I am in Seminary. Consider this a gift. If you are not sick you don't need a doctor. So, you may not need Christ, but I do. I make the decision to follow Jesus, to be a disciple. You can too. All this material stuff is fine, but you cannot take it with you. We cause pain and hurt to each other; we need to confess our sins to God and ask for forgiveness; whatever is burdening you. Ask Jesus to take that burden. There is a big and mighty God who is offering you peace from torment. The Bible is a road map for living. Everything is in there: praise, worship, parenting, marriage, new direction, hate, betrayal and forgiveness. I leave you now. I have no desire to hurt you, to judge you. That is not my business. That is God's business. I am to love you and make disciples of you. I realize I cannot do it alone. May God bless you both and you come to know him intimately."

With that she moves towards the door. The pair looked lost. Whatever the plan, it failed. Like a zombie, Isabella walks behind her. She walks steadily to the elevator. It's then she realizes Keisha is asking if she's okay.

"What was that about. What in the world is going on?"

"Later Key. I want to get out of here then we can talk," said Martha.

She waited impatiently for the elevator, realizing that the Frontes meant to harm her. No wonder she was nervous. It was a definite warning. But thank you, Lord, she chose Psalm 23 and 91. He shall deliver thee from the snare of the fowler and noisome pestilence, even if she doesn't understand everything biblical but if that wasn't a trap then, she shuddered. The elevator came and she got on. She wanted to get away fast. She wanted to put distance between her and the Frontes. She realized they are tormented souls. It must be guilt harnessing their consciences because they knew their son and brother was raping little girls and didn't try to stop him. She preached; it's up to them. She hurried to the subway and ran into Range Wilder. She groans inwardly.

"Are you okay? You seem different from an hour ago."

"I am fine, thank you."

"Are you sure you don't look as you did before? Can I drop you off somewhere?"

"I really appreciate the offer. But the iron horse is just what I need. The rattle and roll is my best option now. I enjoy traveling on public transportation. Bye," she said and he nods.

"Well, can I walk with you to the subway then?" He asked.

"Can I stop you?"

"No." he said smiling

"Didn't think so. You are very persistent, aren't you?"

"In life, persistence pays off. Think of dreams and desires which you need it to propel you forward and attain that dream. If you give up after the first obstacle, you cheat yourself. Think about scientific discoveries; where would we be without them. Think, there would be no subway if Alfred Beach had given up," he said.

"Okay, you made your point. Many of the examples are valid," she said. "Still, I do not know why you choose me to talk with."

"Have you looked in the mirror lately? He asked."

"Why?"

"You are very beautiful. You have beautiful teeth, beautiful smile and those dimples look perfect on you," he said.

"Wow. That was heavy. Thank you. How many other recipients have there been for this observation," she asked, smiling to minimize the barb.

"I have not said that to anyone in years. Plus, I wouldn't say it if it wasn't true."

"Oh, geez, I feel so special," she said, laughing. "Seriously, thank you. You could have been obnoxious. What do investors do on weekends?"

"Alright, go grocery shopping, pick up dry cleaning, watch the game, basketball, baseball, football according to season. I jog early mornings, play a round of tennis, get a rub down, and have breakfast. Right now, I'm waiting on my sister who is coming for a visit since 2:00 pm. That is why I am outside. But once I return from the subway,

I am going to relax and look over some portfolios. She's a notoriously late person," he said.

"What's her name?"

"Raine Duke. She's married. Yes, she has twin girls, Sophia and Sheika. Honestly, I can't wait to see the twins; my sister, not so much," he said.

"Children can be such joy," she said. A vision of Peter floats in her head. Her nostalgic tone and brief flash of pain, let him know she lost a child.

"What happened to him?" he asked gently.

"What? How?" her voice trails off.

"How did I know? Your voice, face, and eyes tell their own story."

"It's a long story and we are at the subway. How is it you offered to take me 'where ever,' and you are expecting company?"

"Because it's long past the time my sister should have been here plus, my nieces would nag if she did wait," he said, smiling. She'd wait for me. Stay safe and safe travels."

"Thank you, have a great visit," she said.

Chapter 3

She is going to WASP. She knows Keisha is pacing and chewing gums waiting for her. Thank heavens it's not cigarettes. In ten minutes, she's on our way from Union Square. She will walk to W 12th quickly. She removes the earpiece. She cannot think about 306 E 94th St. Range is right persistence does give rise to new and innovative ideas and products. Look at the technological advance of today. She remembered visiting Disney World at about age 6 or 7 and saw food growing in water and sand. Now, years later, the vegetables grown are used in their restaurants, or so they claim. She is on autopilot and reaches WASP. Her eyes see very little on the way and she bolts through the door taking the stairs. Predictably, all WASP is there waiting. Heaven knows what Keisha said to them. After hugs all round, Keisha demands to know what is going on.

Martha asks her not to play back the tape. She explains that Mrs. Frontes and daughter Isabella or Bella are concerned she will tell the Judge's secret that he was a pedophile. Once I was behind bars, they were secure, but once I got out, I am a potential threat to them and their secrets.

All that understanding and forgiveness terminated the day I got cleared of all charges, apparently. And the invitation was to use a truth serum on me. Luckily, I saw Isabella drop the pills in my drink. Their behavior, furtive looks, cold eyes and plastic smiles and rehearsed speech put me on my guard. But before I went there, I read Psalm 91 and Psalm 23. My faith saved me. I believe that God would protect me and He did. I feel sorry for them.

"What? Sorry for them, asked Keisha. They tried to hurt you. How did you escape?"

"When they left to get a towel because my drinks spilled. But I poured it on the sofa and cushion so I did not drink it. I just make believe. And then I started preaching to them that was an opportunity to let them know about the love of God and let them know I am studying the word of God, that going to jail is nothing to brag about. What they forget is that there are two persons who are more threatening to them than I am or could ever be. The girl that killed him and his pimp, the one who supplied the girl."

"Oh, goodness, honey, are you okay? said Sasha. Those two must be crazy. What drug do you think they used?"

"More than likely barbiturates. You have contacts you can get it. It's a drug that's supposed to soften you up for interrogation and guys, you will sing like the proverbial canary," said Martha.

"Marty, I am sorry for what happened. Thank the Lord, you are alright. It could easily have gone sideways, said Bethanne. "The duplicity of people!"

"So. Who was that other voice? That I heard in the background," asked Keisha

"Background where?"

"Seems like there was a male voice. I picked up twice when you got off the train, going to and coming from the Frontes," said Keisha!

"Oh. I met this investment broker. He was waiting on his sister and nieces to visit," said Martha.

"I am not really interested in any man," said Sasha. "Those two should be in prison for what they tried to do to you. How can you be so calm about it? I'm fuming."

"Down. Attorney Erin Regan, I know you're the daughter of the Commissioner of Police but hold it there. Yes, the Mama was ingenious, but grief and pain can change reasonable people to irrational fiends.

"Yes," said Bethanne. "They are hypocrites. All that pseudo affection and false sympathy. If I were the target, I would make them pay."

"Well thank heavens it's not you. Please ladies, let it go. It is not worth it. I feel God stepped in. No harm, no foul. I forgive them," said Martha.

"Why are you taking it so lightly? I have everything on tape, even the private conversation in the kitchen. With some enhancement I can make the sound pop," said Keisha.

Okay. Meghee. Miss MIT, I am okay. Yes, so she is not what we expected. Do you remember why King Solomon is known as the wisest one ever lived? Do you remember the classic test of finding the true mother of the baby? Two women lived in a tenement and gave birth at the same time. The first mother's child died, and she switched her dead baby for the live baby. A quarrel developed and they took the case to Solomon; he listened to both, each claiming the child. He said he'd split the baby in two since each claimed the live child. The first mother agreed. The second one didn't agree because that was her child. Solomon knew the second mom was the mother of the live child. What's the relevance? Not so sure but, even though my children are not with me for their sake let it go. I forgive her. There's no evidence she did anything. She can't be held for what she intended to do. I love you all for thinking about me and concerned about me but, we have nothing. And even if there was, I'd do nothing. She is about in her seventies, right? I feel sorry for her. Conscience will be her nemesis," said Martha.

The others exchanged looks. The passion seemed to have gone out of her. For the first time, they noticed the change. It is not physical because she is still beautiful. Pretty teeth and knock out figure; her hair- a luxurious head of hair. She still has the girlish look if you look only at her face, but her hips show maturity, she still turned heads without trying. Sasha looks at her best friend and Gabriel's godmother. He still loves her. Will even hug and kiss her but not her, his mom. It's all about his godmother. They've always shared a special bond. He still will lie in her lap, ignoring he's almost 18 years. She couldn't begrudge the closeness. She is the best godmother and auntie. Charles is just as crazy about her. Those three have a real love fest going on. It is as if she lost her best friend for good; first imprisonment and now her conversion to Christianity. She seems too calm and without fire.

"Okay," said Keisha. I am angry. I can see where the great judge got his chutzpah. The wealthy and well to do always seem to get away with things; anything and everything. See, the great Judge got away with being a pedophile. After all that, got an out. He cheated imprisonment. Put him in Rikers and in general population that would have been justice for all those underaged girls he raped. He got away with it. I'd love a chance to tell that prissy and chick," she said, and snorted.

Martha looked at Keisha. Her face is twisted in anger. Her nostrils are flaring.

"Key honey. I know you are outraged on my behalf. But let time deal with them. It's not easy believing or accepting you gave birth to a sexual predator and deviant. I'll try to reassure her I am not a threat to her or her son's social image. I heard years ago that it's a man's weakness that destroys him and that's what happened to Judge Frontes. Maybe one day she will understand I did not cause his demise, as ironic as it is. I liked him, handsome, well dressed, and well-spoken. Yeah, he had one fatal flaw that ended his journey on this earth. I am learning to forgive and it's hard. But I do not have a choice," she said, hugging Keisha.

Martha notices the tears. There's anguish in her eyes. She has to talk with Keisha alone. She seems to have things bottled up. She seems to be hurting. Martha asks what are their plans for tonight? The two boys are out with school friends with a 10:30 curfew. So, no plans to go out? They decide to order in after much debate ordered Chinese; shrimp and broccoli, egg foo, young, chow fun, chicken fried rice and fried wings for the boys. Sasha asked Martha how was the visit to the park.

"It went well, Peter was there with his friends, the parents and grandma got to meet him. I presumed upon my status as babysitter, showed him my ID, and told him to tell his parents he met me, said Martha.

"Isn't that risky?" said, Melissa.

"How?" asked Martha.

"I don't exactly know. Remember how you used to feel and that's why you gave up babysitting him? I don't want you hurting Marty. It must be so hard on you."

"What are you going to do? Marty. Will you ever tell him? Do you think he has the right to know? What if he meets his sister? Falls in love, get married," said Bethanne.

"Yes, I think about their meeting, but not in those details. It is hard because I believe Doctor Gruniche switched or destroyed the records. How was he able to shoo the others from the delivery room, leaving only himself and Gretchen. It's a difficult decision. I have to think about it. Do you know that's what has plagued me, that there is a brother and a sister out there that does not know the other exists," said Marty. She sighs, then continues, "if I could only find Sarai. I know adoptions are sealed, but wasn't there a case somewhere where a child sued to get the record unsealed. And isn't there something about a good cause to open the records?"

"Yes," said Melissa. "A couple of years ago, New York State passed a law that lets adults over 18 request their original birth certificate. In New York State, the adoptive records are sealed. When the adoption is approved by the court, the adoptive parents are given an adoptive certificate and the new birth certificate with the child's adoptive name and is issued by Department of Health. The children can have the records unsealed for medical reasons or for good cause, courtesy of Google," she said triumphantly.

"Well, said Keisha you forget me. There's no computer door that is closed to me, figuratively speaking, of course. I can sneak in, poke around without being caught. Hey, no judgment. I want to help Peter aka Gabriel meet or find his sister and vice versa."

"I cannot be hearing this. That's breaking and entering, figuratively speaking. I didn't know you envied my incarceration. Considering your outrage a while ago wasn't that the reason you think the Frontes' should pay because I was unjustly convicted?"

"Yes. But that is different. The stakes are too high for these children. They deserve to know each other. Neither one knows he or she is a twin, so they will not be looking."

"I can understand your reluctance, Marty. You, being a Christian and all. I admire you want to walk the straight and narrow, but do not close your eyes to what could happen. When you do not know something, then there's nothing to do but when you do then, you are obligated to do something. Do you know what consanguineous marriage is? In layman's term, marrying cousins. When marriage takes place within the family then there are genetic defects or conditions and a whole lot of mess. If you can stop it, you should. Heaven forbids, because those defects are apparent in their children, then they'll know they married their family member. It's the offsprings that will suffer. Given your delicate conscience, you will be tormented. Find your daughter. Tell Peter. Tell them both. Let them arrange their own meeting if you want to keep out of it. Just saying," said Bethanne.

After Bethanne's speech there is absolute silence. She can be brutally honest, too honest at times. But isn't that why they formed the WASP? Isn't that the mission, to serve and protect. Doesn't that mean their own? The group is lost in silence, each with her own thoughts. What ifs are enemies of peace and your equilibrium.

"Guys. I know you mean well. This I need to pray about. You have valid points, but my decision will be through prayer, fasting and searching the scriptures. The book of Proverbs is an excellent starting point, said Martha. Now where is the food we ordered? She added and simultaneously the doorbell rang. The food is here. As they mix and match their orders, the friends start to joke.

"Key. Remember, don't eat too much. You know that little problem you have, quipped Bethanne.

"What are you talking about? You kiss the boys and make them cry, Nurse," said Keisha.

"You know, for all the years I know you the only place that food goes is in your bum. No diet or exercise ever changed that. So. All that fry and heavy saturated you are gobbling down; I'd ease up if I were you. Just saying," said Bethanne. They all laugh.

"Do not encourage her, she is just envious. I am not going to deprive myself or my palette of the wonderful fare. That will not stop me. My derriere is a gift? Look at all the women running to doctors to give them high tussy or buy pads," said Keisha.

"Y'all are amazing. With all the brain and intellect gathered in this room and that's your topic, tussy. What a stimulating conversation. Do go on. What do they have? platinum or gold?" said Martha."

"Depends on how much you pay for one cheek," said Keisha unrepentant.

There is general laughter.

"Did you stop watching basketball. Who do you think will win this year? Golden State or Lakers, Heats, who? I didn't get to follow up too much, said Martha.

"Frankly. Lakers and Golden State not playing like last year. Steph is invincible to me. I just wait for him to from downtown. It's a most beautiful thing. But it's amazing how King James. keeps going. Man, that's why I believe age is just a number; no one will catch him for points scored. Can you believe it? Nearest person is like what, 10,000 points away? Can scarcely wrap my head around that. I mean, wow.

"Double wow. I remember when he was going for Kareem's record, I could not stand it. That's February 7th. He threw down 38 points, which is amazing, but what I hear, that was amazing seats were going for $20,000 and up. I don't believe that. Really! Love you LeBron, but I'll sooner watch you on TV. Can you imagine? Front row seat in my living room? It is fascinating and horrific at the same time and hopefully rumor," said Shaquana.

"What I find fascinating is that among active players. The closest is Duran and he's over 10,000 points behind. Anyone wanting to attain that record better get recruited at the age of 15 and maybe they'll catch up. You know, Steph and others many times pull something a hamstring here, muscular this or that. They work so hard. That's why I love to watch. I love them guys, but Knicks and Lakers still my team," said Martha.

"How is it you like Lakers?" asked Bethanne.

"My mom loved Lakers. Magic was her guy. Oh, that smile. She said she cried when he retired. She was in bed the whole day. Called in! Magic was Dad's rival. I heard that he said he did not want to win his lady love by default. He wanted to win because he is the better man," said Martha. They all burst out laughing.

"You must have had a great childhood," said Keisha.

"I remember one time my dad bought a pair of slacks. He called. Dor, Dor. Come here. How do I look? Nice, said mom. Dad had a meeting in Manhattan at the Javits Center. He is taking the train. When he came home, he told her Dor, "I still got it. This lady touched me on my buttocks. Yeah. I got it, he said doing the George Jefferson strut. Later that night Mom locked him out. You got the couch, she said. Okay Dor, I ain't got it; ain't got a thing. See nothing! Come on honey, let me in. Just wanted to see if you still love me. Mom didn't answer and he started to sing. When She Was My Girl. He sang so loud that Mom let him in. I know you couldn't hold out. Missed me, did you? Later I heard. Ouch, what was that for. My mom clobbered him. I laughed so hard that night. They're always clowning."

The ladies fall out. They are laughing and rolling on the floor. The phone starts ringing. Martha picks it up. She walks away from the group her back to them. When she comes back, she is smiling.

"Well," said Sasha

"Well, what? No privacy. That's my godson. Can't I speak with my own godson without getting the third degree. He is just checking in, is all," she drawled.

"See. See the difference? Usually, I have to check on him. Because his godmother is here. He calls. You know Marty, you should keep him. Do you know how many years I heard you are only saying that because Auntie Marty is not here. Auntie Marty would not agree with you. Yes, and she wrote to him every month and me her roommate two letters per year. One day I saw him writing a letter, so I stood behind him to see what he was writing, boy told me to give him some privacy. (The ladies are laughing). I guess I'm a slow learner; there's always Auntie Marty. He'll hold her hands and voluntarily kiss her but his mom; oh no. So, at nights for egotistical satisfaction, I kiss him over and over when asleep," said Sasha.

As the others laugh Bethanne said, "Seriously Sasha, you're crazy."

"Maybe but, my friend here doesn't try and he's all over her. But given the way she spoils him, it follows."

"Sasha, please. Don't interfere with me and my godson. He loves his godmother."

"Don't remind me. I was happy to be a substitute for these years. He used to curl up under my arms and cry and then sleep. I felt so sorry for him back then. Still, I had to steal a kiss, Sasha said. And now? They just pick up where they left off. Thick as thieves they are now."

"Never mind, Sash. Your day will come." Said Martha consolingly, kissing her cheek.

"Sure, Marty," she said, without conviction.

They are snickering. Martha goes to the kitchen and returns with individual sparkling ciders. They raise a toast to friendship, health, long life and a bright future in the Lord. Martha invites them to First Presbyterian Church by the corner.

"Come on guys. It's not even a block away and not even an hour and a half service. Come and listen to the word of God. You listen other things," said Marty.

They reluctantly agree. So, what about your nephews?" asked Keisha.

"They are coming with me also. You have neglected my nephew's Christian education. Do you know that the church donates space as PS 3 for special needs children, for autism."

"What? Really!"

"Yes, and they host AAA meetings there and other social services. Remember they used to partner with Lady of Pompeii and Dutch Reformed Church as the caring community and had a Senior Center. I don't know if all that is still going on. We should go because, like everywhere else, I know they suffer much loss due to the pandemic. If you prefer, wear your masks inside. I feel such peace. When I go there. There used to be some sisters who used to attend from whence I knew not, but they seemed frail but pleasant. How about Sister Katherine, Petrona and Father de la Vega? Anyone talk with them recently?"

"We sent cards and gifts last December, but you know they do not accept anything. Then we sent gifts for the girls in the home. Do you know one day I persuaded them to have a meal. They would only have mac and cheese and fish. No excess for them, said Shaquana. Now that was a miracle they accepted. They were kind to us,ot the horror we heard growing up of how mean some of them are and unemotional."

"Amen to that, said Melissa. I have fond memories of them. I've always wondered at the vows they make and keep. Does God sanction that. What do you think, Marty?"

"That's not something I have knowledge of. But if they believe, that's the way to serve their God, as long as it is with truth and honesty and in love it's alright. I was reading James 1 verse. 26 and 27 it states that people who consider themselves religious yet have loose tongues, you know, gossips, malign; basically, have no filter is fooling themselves and their religion is worthless. That religion that God accepts is one that takes care of the sick, the old, the orphans, the widows. And keep themselves from being immersed in the world to stay away from evil. That's my interpretation to that. When I was young, I questioned that and didn't see the logic in it. I believed you could be a Christian with a family. You are not taken into the wilds of the world; where things that are evil, malicious and harmful to others. I still believe that choosing to turn aside from the world for religious reasons is a choice. People choose to start and join gangs; to start crime families and there's nothing noble in those causes. Look at gang initiation. A couple of years ago you had to knock someone out. The nuns are alright with me. They preach and teach the word of God, act with compassion and kindness, love God, self and neighbor that's the commandments," said Martha. My friends Go to King Solomon, the book of Proverbs. It's a little difficult to understand the King James Version, but it's like poetry. The words are magnificent. Proverbs 3 is an excellent description of how to live. Listen to verse 28. Say not unto thy neighbor go and come again, and tomorrow I will give you. When thou hast it by thee. How many times have we done that or know people who have done that? And for no reason except orneriness. Anyway, the good news you have options of new Biblical translations," said Martha

"That is a whole sermon, Marty,". said Shaquana.

"Yes. And read James 1 also. Don't be hearers only, but be doers of the word," said Martha.

A companionable silence lapsed over the group; each WASP lost in her own thoughts. Shaquana's marriage is on the rocks. She is sorry for the outcome of that marriage. She had such hopes. They were so in love when they got married eight years ago. Her first child Kawain is happy with her mother. What is it with the first born? They love their grandmothers fiercely. Sasha, Keisha, Bethanne and Melissa didn't fare much better. Thank heavens she has only a little girl, Zoe. And there she strikes out again. She's a daddy's girl. Can she salvage this relationship or does she want to. She tried for a whole year to get things back, but it seems futile. Intimacy is nonexistent now. It was lukewarm and one night in frustration when Paul sighed and turned to her as if it was a chore, she told him not to bother, it's all right, do not do her any favors. And she turned her back. That sealed it. What had gone wrong in her marriage? They both exist. She remembered the days of the WASP. She manned the station but limited her time there. Of course, she had kept the full truth from him, that WASP worked with unwed mothers stretching the truth, that keeping in touch with Sister Katherine is a constant. She smiles a little sad. Paul is such a disappointment. Thankfully, she's not a sex crazed teenager.

"When am I going to see my niece, Zoe?" Martha asked Shaquana.

"She's with MGM Jennifer; she loves it there. She is getting spoiled by grandma, grandpa, two aunts and an uncle. If I were in her shoes I'd want to be there too. And yes, the adoring older brother! Nobody pays attention to me, so I don't go there very often. I just drop off and pick up," she said.

While the others laugh Martha said, "You make it sound like laundry."

"Feels like it too. Only I drop off clean and pick up dirty. Is all," she said with a shrug.

"So where is Paul when all this is going on; thought he's the doting Papa," said Melissa.

"He is. But he has late hours at work or out with the boys. Then Santa Claus comes in and kisses his daughter and maybe reads her a bedtime story and goes to bed after watching sports."

Despite her lighthearted banter, Martha is suspicious. She feels all is not well Quana.

"Maybe. Marty, you're losing your touch. How is it you haven't tried to inveigle us to play scrabble?" Lissa asked."

"Well. You just asked,' said Sasha. Thus, they begin to play. The game continues until the boys arrive home. After preliminary greetings, Gabriel said, "I smell food. Do you have fried rice with chicken Auntie Marty."

"How many of us are here? And you ask Auntie Marty," said Sasha.

"Oh, mom don't hate. I'm Auntie Marty's favorite. Plus, she misses me. See." he kisses Martha's cheek.

"Of course you are. You are," she said diplomatically.

"Yes, Auntie Sasha, Auntie Marty loves us both. You should see the look of envy we got the other day we were out walking." said Charles.

"So why aren't you happy to walk with me," said Keisha.

"Oh, well because you are mom. Plus, that's not the cool thing to do" he said, grinning cheekily at his mother. Martha heats the food in the microwave for the boys and joins them at the table.

"So how did things go today?" she asked."

"Everything went okay. We had a good time eating pizza, playing touch football and later video games," said Gabriel.

"Yeah, Antonia's Papa was out but his mom is really cool. She's a part time Legal secretary. She gave Antonio her credit card to order whatever we wanted. The pizza wasn't that good, but the bread sticks were," said Charlie.

"Hope you two boys know you are showering before bed with all that sweat and junk on you, said Sasha.

"Mom, how do you know we are smelly? Auntie Marty is right by me and she's not complaining."

"Well, son, Auntie Marty has blocked nostrils. Gabe, you will shower, especially since Auntie's taking you to church tomorrow. Scrub behind your ears really good, then you'll have very little to do to get ready," said Sasha.

Gabriel appealed to Martha.

"It's not punishment honey. Bathe tonight you so can sleep until 8:30, if you need breakfast. Then we go to church. It's just down the block. You know First Presbyterian Church service starts at 9:00, ends at 10:15. Then we can go to Mickey D's or The Grill for a greasy breakfast," said Martha.

The boys brighten but none of the adults is fooled. They are not excited about church. Greasy breakfast is the incentive. They elect to stay with Martha with their parents rolling their eyes.

"Isn't it amazing? Labor and delivery mean nothing to children. No gratitude. Grandma is their favorite or daddy, godmothers and aunties and mothers last," said Keisha.

Martha refuses to take the bait and gives them a wide-eyed innocent stare. She knows just how to madden Sasha and Keisha. She always takes up for the boys even since they were toddlers. She felt it her duty to let them feel they were losing their minds, although truthfully, the boys were a pleasure to babysit. She never had the problem their mothers did. They accused her back then, as they do now, she spoils them. Well, maybe just a little. "Okay, you are not delinquents. Find your clothes for church. There are no excuses."

"Oh boys, you are my friend. And I am asking, it's good to go to the House of the Lord and worship him. Be with the people of God and you will enjoy a live sermon for a change. Always the music is wonderful. That beautiful pipe organ must be heard. Oh, it's wonderful. You'll be blessed,' said Martha.

"Okay, I'll go," said Keisha. And to the others, "you are coming too."

"Seriously, ladies. There is much for me to give God thanks for on so many levels. Do you know I could have been killed in prison? Do you know the level of violence in that prison? That day I was attacked, but for the mercy of God I am alive. It's the same bullies you meet in junior high and high school. Think I didn't want to retaliate? I was there for a crime I didn't commit, so I didn't want to commit one in there. She didn't know I knew she had attacked me. That's why I rolled away so she wouldn't stomp my face. I protected my chest too. I have to serve God. There are no doubts. Then you had the guards I dispatched, reason I was beaten up. They preyed on some women forcing sex on them for favors. I told the warden about that ring. A sexual predator inside a prison wall or outside is still a predator and worst you are bombarded with sexual advances by females as well as male. I was singled out as 'preppie'. And for the male guards to rub on me; or make crude gestures at other times. One time I was called from the yard to take over duties in the common room. I should go pick up the list from the supervisor. When I got there, he locked the door, barred the way and started his lewd talk. He said he had wanted to help me out as he helped the others. It's a great sacrifice, but he's willing to give it to me. What is it you have that you think I want? I asked him. I hear you haven't got any and I want to give it to you. Don't play coy, I feel like you need it or are going the other way. Thank you for your generosity, but I am fine. I will pass. He would not stop. I'm praying Lord help me because I don't want to kill. He came at me trapping me and I let him get close and I gave him a knee right in the 'c'. He doubled over. I called two other guards and let them see him in pain.

Later, the warden returned. I went to him. I sought refuge in the Infirmary. That's how it happened. They cleaned house. Do you know how angry and bitter I was? I was consumed with anger and bitterness about all these sexual predators, men, women, the gangs, yet it's a mild facility, it is said. I heard too it was a special favor I was placed there and not a maximum secure facility. I wondered if it was the Judge mother's influence. So, I have to practice forgiveness, or else I'd look for the quack I had for a lawyer, the detectives that didn't do their jobs, people in the crime lab, because I had the time to research bomb making or such device. I need God. I need God to cleanse my soul. And to soften my heart. Resentment is a pillow that refreshes hatred and keeps it burning. So, I read through all Saint Paul's struggles and listen to King Solomon. These are my guide and encouragement. I embrace the first commandment, love God and my neighbor as myself. If I let it, it will overwhelm me. But I pray every chance I get. That's why I can have some peace. I must forgive."

"Oh Marty! Sasha hugs her openly crying, Keisha and Bethanne sniffling. And the WASP gathers in a group hug each seeking solace from the other. Their fierce, passionate Marty had suffered atrocities they could not fathom; literally sleeping and watching at the same time.

She is sorry for unloading on them unlike previous conversation. Keisha's reaction to Mrs. Frontes and the Judge shows bitterness and unforgiveness even if it was on her behalf. She understands it but she knows without constant work will become bitter. She must remind herself without forgiveness she will not be whole. She cannot do it alone so listening to Ms. Joyce Myer, who was sexually abused by her father, forgave him. She even took care of him in his latter years.

"Okay, what? We go to church tomorrow. We have much to be grateful for: love of God, love of self, of families and friends. They dispersed to Keisha's apartment to sleep and some at Martha's apartment aka WASP HQ. Naturally, the two boys stay with Martha, Keisha, Shaquana and Melissa leave. The boys will use the bunk bed and the three will share the bedroom. They all set off for church at 8:45 AM. They want to be there before the choir gets in procession. Luckily, they can enter the side door. Martha always liked the aisle seat to hear the different sections of the choir. First Presbyterian has a wonderful choir. She'd go there just to hear the choir and the pipe organ. She likes the organ prelude as well. As the WASP enter the church with the two young men, heads turn; they make a statement. Each WASP looks confident, self-assured, polished; but looks are deceiving. They are ushered to an empty pew. In fact, they need two so Keisha and Sasha sit together. There's shuffling because Charles and Gabriel want to sit beside Martha. She changes places so she is between both of them.

Keisha said to Martha, "Even in church you spoil them."

Martha smiles and makes a face at her as she kisses both boys on the cheek to their delight and the chagrin of their mothers. As the prelude ends, the pastor begins. 'This is the day that the Lord has made. We will rejoice and be glad in it'. The organ roars and there are two trumpeters. Wow, what a treat. Martha is so caught up in the atmosphere it's like a light is turned on inside her. Oh heavens! The opening hymn is Praise My Soul, The King of Heaven, and she is transported. She sings lustily, oblivious to everything around her. She missed the look of wonder and surprise on the boys' face. They join in the singing. They have heard trumpets before but not like this. When they were younger, they had band at school but had no aptitude for violin or cello. But if someone had played the trumpet like this, they would have stayed in band. The sermon is as impressive as the singing. An usher asks the visitors to sign the book, she looks at Martha.

"You have been here before. Thank you for coming back. You can make this your church home. We would love to have you all, her smile is bright. She introduces herself as Laurie Baxter and shakes their hands. She tells them of coffee hour on the second floor.

"Do you have bacon and eggs?" said Charles, hopefully.

Laurie laughs. "Nothing so sumptuous young man, just tea, juice, coffee, cookies, maybe muffin buddies. But it is certainly wonderful to see you young men. Hope you come again. There's a young people's group and if you want, you can even join the choir." Both boys exchanged looks and grins.

"We could if you want to get rid of the members. Not our talent. We only sing at home to punish our moms and siblings," said Charles laughing.

"Please don't let that stop you. Come again," said Laurie.

"Can we find a breakfast buffet," said Charles.

"I don't know where any is. "We may have to go to Union Square," said Martha.

With cell phone in hand, the boys find Big Buffet in the West Village. Melissa tells them they cannot go because her shoes are not made for walking. So, they can go to The Grill on 13th St. otherwise they will have to carry her home.

"Let's go to The Grill, then. Ok guys, next time we go big buffet on a Saturday when we are alone," Martha tells them.

"Hey, I hear that," said Keisha.

"Hear what?" Martha asked innocently. I went to church because of breakfast. Promise, even if it was a great sermon.

She said: "I have two children to feed. The rest of you are on your own. Breakfast is for the children. Unless of course, you are children." They said yes. Martha and the boy's laugh.

"Okay, children. Let's go. We will breakfast at The Grill. Hope it's not too crowded since it's breakfast till 2:00 PM. They find a baguette and the waitress takes the order. The boys want the 'Big Breakfast,' Bacon, sausage, eggs, home fries and bagels with orange juice. The WASP orders sausage, bacon, toast, coffee, herbal tea. When all the breakfast is served, they hold hands and pray, they use sanitizer, then eat. Martha watches her nephews sweet talk, the waitress into giving extra home fries and scrambled eggs. She laughs because they are slender when she asks where all the food goes, they shrug, saying it goes in their growing. They are about 5 feet 8 inches.

"You have a point there in your growth. That's a good place for it anyway. After such a big breakfast, you don't need dinner, right?" said Martha.

"You wish," said Sasha.

"Really wishful thinking," said Bethanne and laughed. "Thank heavens it doesn't show because if it did you would have to gather them in installments. "

There is general laughter, but Charles asks, "what do you mean Auntie?"

"Well, if all the food you eat consolidates and you become very fat then we would have to hug you a little at a time; your right side then your left then your back. That's installment."

"Do you know I saw a young guy at T Mobile store. He was so huge I'm sure his mother has to hug him in installment," said Charles.

"Why do you think he is like that and for all the oversize people," said Gabe.

"Okay nurse, the balls in your court," said Sasha.

"It's not any one thing- It can be very complexed. Not all plus size or obese people overeat. Some people have overactive thyroids, could be medication used to treat depression/anxiety; asthmatics treated with steroids, compulsive eaters and we cannot forget our gluttons. Also, people with down syndrome it is said, are two times more likely to have obesity and four times more likely to have extreme obesity. This can be for physiological reasons- slow or low metabolic rate, low energy and minimal physical activity and unhealthy diet. That's in a nutshell but it's a lot. For that reason, we should not judge or be quick to judge. That's why Eunice Kennedy worked with special needs children and got them involved with athletics. It gets the children to train and conditioning. Now that's enough for today."

They finish their breakfast, and Martha declares she is going to get food, because she is going to cook for the boys.

"My goodness! What a surprise. She does not miss a beat-totally dedicated to her nephews. They are the VIPs of 71 W12th," said Melissa.

"Please stay out of my business. My nephews are important to me; to love up on them before I go back to work. I'll be teaching them to cook today," said Martha.

They pick the meat; oxtail and salmon, carrots, fresh string beans, red kidney beans, coconut milk, gravy master, onions and garlic. At home the meat is cleaned and seasoned and put to marinate, meanwhile string beans are cleaned likewise the carrots. Some of the carrots are cut in chunks and placed in a pot to partially cook and blend with condensed milk, vanilla and dark sugar. The other portion they will be blend with ginger and lime juice, sugar free. While they work Martha tells them of the goodness of God. She asks both if they believe in a sovereign God. Charles shrugged he does not believe fully because so many bad things happen; the murder of children in Connecticut and Florida. Gabriel is skeptical too because good people get hurt.

"Look at you Auntie. Why did He take you from me. Why were you locked up," said Gabriel tears rolling down his cheeks. She hugs him.

"Yes, bad things happen to good people, and it is unfortunate. It is the evil of men's heart. God does not cause it; He gives us free will to choose. Mankind makes choices good and bad. This morning you wanted the big breakfast; that was your choice. Your mom and I allowed you to have it, we did not stop you, but you could've changed your mind. When we asked if you were sure, you said yes. God talks to us, but we ignore him because of disobedience. You hear many times someone say my mind was telling me not to, but I did anyway. We ignore God's voice. Don't you think the boy in Connecticut knew the gun shots would kill his classmates? And the one in Florida went to McDonalds to eat after he murdered his classmates. These are people devoid of conscience even if they say they have mental issues. There is evil and they personify evil. And people who say its guns that kill are disingenuous. A gun in a drawer does not have the ability to shoot/murder anyone but someone has to take it out, load it and pull that trigger. I tried to save the Judge's life but didn't. I saw the person and it's crazy to try reason with a person with a knife intent on hurting someone else. Some lessons are very hard, like mine. Now when we have people who do not work with integrity, fail to do their jobs properly, are lazy, dishonest and set people up, then what happened to me will keep happening to others. And it is wrong every day. I saw this man on AGT spent who forty years in prison for something he did not do. However, He kept me and is helping me to forgive those who contributed to my incarceration. I still believe in the goodness of God. Look, what a beautiful place he gave us to live, and we destroy it with pollution. He keeps us so we can turn to Him and trust Him; to live as He taught and still teaches us to love him and your neighbor as yourself. She shares Galatians 5: 22 – 23 the fruits of the spirit; assures them it takes more restraint to refrain than to retaliate.

The boys learn how to cook oxtail by braising and the salmon by broiling. The oxtail is tender, except for the bones of course, and salmon flaky and well-seasoned. They mix garlic, butter and lemon juice and pour it over the salmon for taste and to lessen the scent of fish. The boys boast about their cooking and Gabriel said he could beat Bobby Flay and Gordon Ramsay. Dessert is served when the kitchen is cleaned, and plates are washed. They have ice cream and fruit cocktail. They chat for a while and then get ready to leave. They pray, making a circle before going home. She ends; May the God of Isaac and Jacob watch over you. After they leave, Martha sits with her Bible to study, but her unruly thoughts intrude. She wonders if she could have given a more substantial explanation of free will; that ultimately whatever we do is a choice. The very next lesson for the boys will be about choice.

She is glad they did not ask about helping others. Should you help because it's convenient to do so. It's ironic because that's what led to her arrest and subsequent incarceration. For a long time, she swore she would never help like that again. She will give coffee to someone, pick up a bag, but not help a wounded person. Unwittingly, the parable of the Good Samaritan came to mind. She said outraged, Shut up, mind. Who asked you? Her instincts would take over anyway. She's not mean and that's why she's a work in progress. She remembered her Jamaican godmother telling her a story. Her brother Derrick told her while driving around Junction, this man's truck broke down. He lifted the hood and tried to fix it. He moved the cap to the radiator and the water spewed out and burnt him. Derrick coming up saw the man the c and wanted to help him. He knew he had to get the man out of the T shirt because that held the hot water. But when he ran for his machete then he said what if the police should come around the corner and see me with a machete in my hand and thinks he was actually hurting this man? They would shoot him. So, for a while he didn't do anything and worse because the man was crying so loud. Help! Help! Help! He told the man don't cry so loud. I am going to help you; finally got the courage to get behind him and slit the T shirt. She smiles at the memory. So, we all have choices to make. What we do, how we do, when we do. She got back to studying Matthew chapter 13:10 to 30. She marvels at all that involves planting the seed, which is the word of God. It sets you up for growth, caring, weeding and change.

She has a dream. She's in Prospect Park. There's a teenage girl and boy walking, holding hands. Around the park are patches of quilts filled with children and adults having picnics. It is a perfect day. As her eyes roam, she's admiring that landscape, her eyes returned to the boy and girl. She was struck by the girl's posture. Shoulders back, head erect. She is slim, has a tiny waist and nice flare to the hips. She wonders what she looks like, and simultaneously she stops and turns around. Martha's breath is caught. She is a beautiful creature, even at a distance. As in a trance, Martha watches as they walk towards her. She closes her eyes. The girl is familiar, but where has she seen her? As they come closer, she sees the perfectly arched brows, long lashes, lips outlined with dark lip liner and delicate pink lipstick, but no other evidence of makeup. She must have been gaping and daydreaming at the same time because she heard. Are you okay? You look shocked. Martha exhales and nods.

The boy said, "Why are you looking at her like that? She's not that way. You must be full of woman love. Back off lady."

For a few minutes she's lost then realizes what the boy is saying. She looks at him and wonders what the heck she sees in him. A ragamuffin with big sagging pants and semi exposed! He sees her looking at him adding, "And I'm not available either," he said. Martha grins to hide her derision. As a teen, she never liked saggy pants where the split and underwear are exposed. That is why Ogwin was so appealing. He was covered. She is a beautiful girl with poise. Her parents must be very proud of her.

"Are you still in high school?" she asked the girl.

"No, I graduated last year. I'm going to New York University. Why?"

"You remind me of someone. Do you live in Brooklyn?"

"Yes and no. I float between Brooklyn and Westchester. My parents are in Westchester. But my grandparents live in Brooklyn. Sometimes it's easier to travel from Brooklyn."

Martha laughs, "you love that iron horse, do you?"

"Wouldn't miss it for the world," she said, smiling. And there it was, the dimples. Martha is struck again.

"Nice talking to you, Miss?" she said.

"Martha. she replied. And what is your name?"

"I am Maya."

Then she jumps out of her sleep. The sound of a truck backfiring disturbs the air. What a dream. She remembered it clearly, but who did the girl look like? Eventually falling back to sleep, restlessly. Later that morning, as she sets off for Colombia, the dream is foremost in her mind. She'd enrolled in an accelerated program for six weeks, equivalent to a semesters work. She's not worried about the speed of the class or volume of the work if she keeps up. With the three weeks she's free before she starts working, it will be only three more weeks to go. For some unknown reason she is unable to focus on her reading. She is restless, she mutters Psalm 23 and 139. But is it true? I can't see the green pasture and there is no still water. And whether I flee from thy presence if I ascend in heaven, you are there, in hell You are there. And if I fly to the sea, you are there. So why can't I feel you, Lord? I am disturbed in my mind. Where are you? I need to feel you. I need you now, Lord, you are silent. Help me. She rests her head on her desk. She must have dozed off because she hears: "Behold, I am with you, even to the ends of the earth. Arise, you have work to do. Go find her as in your dreams today."

What? Find who? I don't know what you are talking about."

"The girl, find her, she needs you." Martha jumps up and looks around, she sees the back of a figure in ecru. She rushes to the door. The hall is empty. She runs to the left and sees a group of students and asks if a tall gentleman passed by them, they said no, she goes the other way and sees no one. Well, she must have dozed off and was dreaming.

She goes back to her seat and picks up her book. 'Thy rod and thy staff, they comfort me,' she repeats in her mind. What strangeness is this besetting her. It is a good thing that others cannot see my thoughts or mind. She can imagine them taking her to Bellevue for psych evaluation. It is weird that the person tells her to go find her. Who is her and what of the back of the person she saw exiting the classroom. Thank heavens for her sobriety. She smiles, shaking her head. And as the words go find her comes again, she says out loud. Get thee behind me, Satan. Find somewhere else to rest. And she focuses on the chorus Heavenly Sunshine. It is a beautiful day. And with that, her spirit lifts.

For three nights, she has the same dream. She is in Prospect Park and she's looking at the beautiful landscape. The last time the young girl is alone, she catches a glimpse of her walking towards the carousel. She runs to catch up with her.

"Hi. Do you remember me?"

"Yes, she said pleasantly. I saw you that day on the other side of the park by the pond."

"Right, said Martha. What is your name?"

"Maya," she said.

"I like that name. Your parents like Maya Angelou," she probed gently.

"Maybe. I believe my mom does. However, I like Amanda Gorman. She's really good."

"Yes, she is excellent. It's great poetry. It's modern and it's very much a part of our legacy. Oh, where is your friend?"

"Friend? Oh, you mean Kenny? I don't really know, that is not my concern anymore. We are not on the same page, so I just told him don't visit anymore. Let's just be casual acquaintances."

"How do you feel about that decision? You miss him? Are you hurting?" asked Martha.

"Do you miss a zit?" asked Maya with a smile.

Martha laughs. "Guess not." Martha looks at her closely and sees the shadows in her eyes. "Are you okay other than the breakup? You have shadows in your eyes. You should have joy and laughter. A burden shared is a load divided."

She inhales and there is real pain. She hugs herself. Varying emotions flit across her face. Martha could see her indecision and gives her, her number to call if she wants to share/ talk. Martha is careful not to ask for Maya's number. "What's your name?" asked Martha.

"Maya Sturgeone," she said.

"Well. Take care of yourself and remember anytime, call," said Martha.

Maya walks away, glances back, and waves. Martha is struck by her. She senses something is wrong, but she cannot force confidence. Maya has to want to do so. Martha awakes, feeling a sense of urgency. She has classes from 9:00 to 12:00. And she will head straight to Prospect Park. She is on assignment. The dreams are not accidental. Of course she cannot tell just anyone. They'd think she needed psychiatric help. She knows it's not her fertile imagination. The gentleman from yesterday gave her a message and assignment. Now she has full name and an image in her head for identification. Maybe she could hire someone to find her. Prospect Park is big and crowded. Well, if she's on assignment, the Spirit will lead her, right? Oh, thou of little faith, she says to herself. She will stand at the carousel. She will get the B or Q trains to Prospect Park. She will enter on the Ocean Ave. side and will begin her search. Martha walks around for more than forty minutes without seeing Maya. She sits near the carousel, her second time visiting there. Well Lord, here I am. I have been looking without success. Please direct me. Which way to go next? There is a class, maybe Grade 3 or Grade 4 by the carousel. There seems to be about twenty children. Half gets on the others get off. She watches idly as the children scream and laugh. She smiles in reminiscence.

"It's sure funny, isn't it? But that was a long time ago," a voice said. Martha looked around to see a mature gentleman in shades watching her. She glances up and smiles and nods. Another time she wouldn't mind the conversation, but she's on assignment. She looks at her watch. Where is Maya?

"Waiting for someone," he asked.

"Yee's. she said, not elaborating. Maybe she can get rid of him by telling him she is directed by the Spirit, just maybe he'd go away. As the mischievous thought enters her mind she smiles.

"Must be someone very special," he said fishing.

Martha turns to him. "Really?" with eyebrows raised.

And he laughs displaying even white teeth. "Okay, I know when I'm not wanted, just wanted to say I saw and spoke to a beautiful woman today, even if she shot me down like Icarus," he said.

"Seriously. Greek mythology. I don't see you flying. I don't see any wings, no sun."

He smiles, "Well, at least you know your myths."

"As you said, it was a long time ago," said Martha.

"Touche! By the way I am Adrian Boone," he extends his hand.

She shakes his hand, "Martha Chimes."

Another time, another place, she'd definitely converse with him but she's anxious. Her impatience must've shown on her face because he said, "I am sorry to disturb you."

"Mr. Boone I am sorry I am distracted. I am waiting for someone, and I am anxious."

"How foolish of me to think you are unattached," he smiles wryly.

"And it's not what you think," she tells him.

"No? But it's rude of me to intrude anyway."

"I am waiting for a young girl. I believe she needs help and I'm waiting to see her. She's average height, brown skinned, full eyes, slim smallish face about size 3/4. That's why I am here," she said.

He looks at her levelly. He sees earnestness and shadows in her eyes. "What if she doesn't come today?"

"I'll come back until I find her," said Martha softly.

Adrian Boone smiles and said, "I am sure you will."

After Adrian Boone leaves, she sits for another fifteen minutes then walks among small groups of people. She walks towards the cycle track and around towards the pond. She smiles, first she is restless for unknown reason, then she gets directions and now she is anxious. She inhales deeply and continues past the pond. She goes up a little slope and to the level where you can see the B68 bus and there sits Maya. She is returning a ball to the toddler. Martha is surprised. She is the exact replica of the girl in her dream. She is unprepared for her own reaction. She is so emotional she cannot speak. But what is she to say.

Lord please do not desert me now, she mutters. Here she is alive. What if nothing is wrong with her. Now she is having doubts. And then she hears Jim Reeves, Thank the Lord and begins to sing the chorus:

O yes, we thank the Lord for every flower that blooms, birds that sing fish that swim and the light of the moon

We thank everyday as we kneel and pray when she is interrupted.

"Do you know my grandmother used to sing that song all the time. It is a lovely song but, there are more words to that right? You sing very well," said Maya.

"Why thank you. I used to hear my Nana sing it too, and grandpa. Yes. She always says people don't thank God enough for the simple everyday things like the air we breathe, or the sunshine. Maybe the farmers are more grateful for the climatic changes," said Martha.

"Yes. Today is beautiful. Blue skies, few clouds, a breeze, it's not sweltering, babies and flowers, dogs, women, children, everybody's out," she said.

"Is that your family?" Martha asked and she shakes her head. May I sit."

"Sure of course. I am taking a break from walking." She is dressed in tights.

"Where do you live asked Martha. Oops! You don't have to answer that."

"That's okay. I live in Park Slopes. By the way I am Maya."

Martha almost passed out. She schools her features and says, "Nice to meet you, Maya. I am Martha."

"This is my favorite haunt. I used to be by the pond with a friend but, needed a change today," said Maya. I always find it peaceful, maybe because of the slope on this side of the pond, it seems that people do not congregate as much. It suits me though."

Martha nods. What can they talk about. Sometimes you just want to be quiet and not engage in conversation with a stranger. But she asked, "do you have another hobby other than walking/ hiking?"

"I like dancing and reading. For five/six years I attended Dance Theatre on Coney Island Avenue. I stopped going about five years ago. I broke my ankle, and it was hard, balancing on my toes after that, and I stopped. I am no Misty Copeland. I did pop but it wasn't the same. I started ballroom dancing one day per week at the Turner Studio. It's easier on my ankles, and that is why I walk. P T said if you can't do the scheduled exercise walk. Anyway, I love being slim. If I have to take off, I'm gone like the wind."

"Really. Now what makes you think of that?" Martha laughs.

"One day when I was very young seven/eight a dog bit Sherry. We were coming home from school, and we saw this dog. As we drew a breast of him, he started to growl. We started running. Sherry was plump and could not go as fast and the dog bit her on the buttocks. Never forget it. Poor Sherry was teased. Tried to get her to stop eating too much jelly donuts, twizzles, jellybeans to no avail. She always ate chocolate cake and ice cream and just waddled along. I just walked on the other side of the road. That is why I only like small dogs like poodles, Pomeranian, Yorkshire Terrier, Cocker Spaniel. The Dachshund is weird looking, don't like the Pug either and the Pekingese looks like it's a child worst nightmare," she laughs.

"You seem to know a lot about dogs. Have you ever had one?" asked Martha.

"I had a cocker Spaniel but he died at age 14. I cried so hard my parents would not buy me another. Now I love the dogs on my block; the nice ones I mean. My parents used to tell me about Lassie. I saw an old re-run one day. My parents were so happy they got popcorn, sparkling cider, cheese, hamburgers and ice-cream. It was fun to see them so excited. Of course I had to be there. They needed a chaperone," said Maya with a cheeky grin.

"Wow! So did you enjoy it," asked Martha.

"Yes. I did. I was a bit distracted. My parents were whispering and talking soft. Mom was giggling – Dad kissing her. I finally figured out why grandma offered to take them to the movies. Those two have no behavior," said Maya.

Martha laughs. "Oh, I see. You seem to get along with your parents. That is very nice. Are you an only child?"

"No but I might as well be. I have a younger sister and brother. They are about seven years my junior. I was so excited when I became a big sister. But now they are brats. Any rotten thing you can imagine or think about they do. And untidy! I bar them from my room," she said.

"What are their names?"

"Wolverine and Chilly Willie," Maya said. However, their parents call them Macee and Darren. Even if they don't look like aliens, they behave like aliens. I've often wondered if mom brought home the right children from the hospital. They are such terrors," she said but looking pleased.

Martha laughs, "I think I can just see how annoying they are to you."

Maya eyes twinkle like stars. She loves her siblings.

Martha looks closely at Maya and sees the shadows in her eyes once she stopped smiling. She is hoping that God gives her a clue. She can sense turmoil amid the lightness of Maya's voice. It's as if she's hiding something. Martha decides she is diving in, head first.

"Maya, I know we just met, and you don't know me, but I do not think it's accidental. I was directed to find you. You are beautiful, congenial, funny. But I notice you grimace and wince at times. I can sense you are in pain. What is it? Can I help you?

"Really. You are imagining things. You are right though we do not know each other. I am fine, Martha," said Maya.

"Alright I know how this must sound and seem strange, but please take my number. If you believe I can help, please call me." Maya hesitates, and Martha reiterates. "I will leave it to your discretion without pressure. I will not ask for your number, but please let me see you save my number. I also need you to promise to call day or night if the need arises."

"What are you, my fairy godmother?" she asked. "I am okay I tell you; I do not need your help. I am fine."

"Before you go, I would like to say a blessing: (And prayed Numbers 6: 24 – 26). The Lord blesses you and keep you. The Lord makes his face shine upon you and be gracious to you. The Lord lifts up his countenance upon you and give you peace. Amen. Go in peace, God will protect you."

As they part, Martha feels no satisfaction. She's not sure what revelation she expected, but she has to be content. Maya doesn't need her help now.

Chapter 4

***

*L*ord, I went to the park, I found Maya. I feel there is something else I should do but don't know what. There is a vast silence. To lift her spirits, she finds Cece Winan's All My Life You Have Been Faithful. You'd think the way she loves that song she would know the title. YouTube helps her out and she starts to sing with Cece. She allows the words to infuse her mind and spirit. After Cece sings to her for the third time, gets a call and heads for the train. She will transfer at W4 for the F. As she walks home, she hopes Keisha is home. Keisha has not returned her text and if she is not there she is going to Nana.

"Key, you home?" she asks as she enters Keisha's apartment.

"In the bathroom, washing off 6th Avenue dust off me. How was school?"

"Wish it was over. I just have two more tests and a paper and I am done, d o n e. I just can't wait. How was your day, and where is my nephew?"

"Being spoilt by his grandmother. It's his cousin Gerald's birthday. They are having pizza party from 5-9. Gerald didn't want to wait until Saturday. He has a game and so I am free."

Martha sits in the sofa and takes out her note book. People in ancient times behave pretty much like now. Prejudice was ripe back then. Jews have no dealing with Samaritans, but they are all Jews separated by history and finance. Jesus himself dealt with that. Can anything good come out of Nazareth? Likewise, his disciples, poor coarse fishermen, tax collector not well learned not a Scribe or Pharisee. That's why she is fascinated with the question of who is my neighbor. Who indeed! There was a lively discussion in class and the parable of the Good Samaritan was the star of that discussion. How many times have we been the Levite, the priest. That stopped many in class. On your way to church you had a flat, earlier accident on the parkway so traffic is backed up; do you stop to help someone lying on the sidewalk. There were cultural norms, societal, economical and even social norms. What of conscience and humanity; was it acceptable to leave it for someone else to do. Martha smiles as she remembers the debate that raged in class. Well, that is why to be His disciple there are neither Jew nor Greek, neither bond nor free, male or female for we are one in Christ. Until people accept Galatians 3: 26-28, there will be controversy the professor ended.

By this Keisha emerges in shorts and top. She kisses Martha. "You hungry? I have only left overs."

"No, I am not hungry. Food has not crossed my mind in a while. I overlooked something when I was incarcerated, my concern to a great extent was for the children and WASP. To protect WASP, I kept you all away wouldn't let you visit- even to writing to me. That was not the right thing to do. I only realized that day I went to see Mrs. Frontes. You were so angry. You were so upset and I thought about it later. I am so very, very sorry."

Keisha's eyes look glassy as Martha hugs her.

"I was so afraid for you. I could not understand why you were so casual about it. I kept thinking they could've hurt you. I don't think I could go through another hurt like that. Even now I shudder when I remember it," she said.

As the friends embrace Martha sighs and states: "I am staying. Here for good. I've listened to many preachers and seminarians, and forgiveness is a big part of our lives on this earth. It is said to forgive quickly, or it festers and grows and we hang on to the pain and hurt that it consumes us. We forgive for ourselves, not for the other person, because if the injury was deliberate or done out of malice, it will return to that person. And the Bible says vengeance is mine, says the Lord I will repay. I believe since God seesand knows everything. You won't lose a thing. God will bless you in your going out and you're coming in. That train that should have left at 8:05. It's still there at 8:08, so you make it. Or the person on line pays for your coffee and bagel because you actually left your purse. Don't worry about that person who hurt you, don't detract from your blessing with unforgiveness."

"I am working on it," Keisha says.

"Okay. But I feel sorry for her. You know you gave birth to such a deviant is not easy. If she turned a blind eye those years before, then that's on her. But if she tried, urged and begged and tried to get him professional help, then she should take comfort in that and ask for forgiveness. If she withheld information from the authorities that she could have stopped it, that's between her and God. You must ask for forgiveness. Acknowledge you are a sinner. If you ask God in sincerity and are willing to change from constantly sinning against God, breaking his commandments, you can be sure salvation is yours. Have a change in heart, see each other as God's children. Be true to God, live a life that people will know you are a disciple of Christ. How you live can start and carry a whole conversation."

"I hear you, but she tried to hurt you. With that, what's its name drugs. You were lucky on Saturday. Said Keisha, unwilling to forgive Mrs. Frontes.

"Remember the hymn says the vilest offender who truly believes is pardoned immediately. Remember, the thief on the cross repented and Jesus told him, 'Today you will be with me in paradise.' I have to be worthy of who I am to Christ. I can't profess the name of Jesus and practice unforgiveness or do lawless things. I can't afford to let anyone say she's a Christian and act like that. We are called to be the light of the world not a stumbling block. Our lives should not hinder others nor lead them away from the Kingdom. I don't want to be a closet Christian or a church Christian. I have to embody the whole life. The Bible says go out into the world and preach the gospel. Tell of the good news. The road to real happiness is living a life that's pleasing to God. Every civilization that I've ever read or heard about believed in a higher source or higher power outside of themselves. And whether you call him God, Jehovah, Yahweh, it's still the Supreme Being. You come to this knowledge through faith, reading and meditation on the Word of God. In the meantime, ask for understanding. It is said Old Testament is prophecy, and the New Testament is the revelation."

"Okay. Reverend Marty Chimes. I understand you are passionate about Christianity," said Keisha.

"It's not only that Key. Look, when we find a nice store, buy a beautiful dress or shoes, we share it, right? So why shouldn't we share the good news of the gospel. We share material stuff; picture of a dog, a new pizza place, why not that Jesus, the Son of God, came to earth to live among us, to be our example, to experience humanity. So, he knows the trials we are faced with, the temptation, the pain of loss, grief. He had friends, Pumpkin. He cried when Lazarus died, but he raised him. Why? Because he has the power over death and the grave. He gives life and continues to do so."

"Gosh Marty, you are studying your Bible. I know about Lazarus being raised from the dead and I always wonder about that," said Keisha.

"Jesus raised Lazarus, but he can perform a miracle now and raise someone else. But we need faith and belief. What I learned is that Jesus called Lazarus by name, or else all the other dead people would have woken up too. Jesus demonstrated he is God. He has power to give life. In the broadest or narrowest of concepts He is Lord, He is sovereign. He has power over life, death and the grave. That's why he died, to save us from eternal death. When he died, death had no more power over mankind, if we are believers. The Bible says death is swallowed up in victory. That's what Jesus' death is to set us free from sin, so we have eternal life. Remember, the dead in Christ will rise just like how he rose from the dead. Yes, O death where is thy sting? Anyway, I do not want my sisters and friends not to experience the love of God and not to love Him. We should all be part of his Kingdom to follow him. It will be glorious, my sister. We are going to have regular Bible study, I'm sure of it.

"Slow down, Evangelist Marty. Do we get a vote?"

"Yes and no," said Marty." Yes, we are going to have a vote, but it's a formality. I will do my best to lead my nephews to be crusaders, so even if you vote nay, I will be the tiebreaker, right?" said Martha complacently to which Keisha rolled her eyes. Martha called each WASP they meet on Friday. On Friday, Martha offers a proposal to the group with the condition they cannot eat her food and do not participate in the discussion nor, fall asleep immediately after.

"What?" said Melissa. I was so looking forward to eat and snooze."

"Well, 'unlook' that desire. Aint gonna happen darling," said Martha pleasantly.

"Well Steph, help me out her Beth?"

"I am getting a small seven inch for myself. Sorry Melissa, pizza wins," said Steph.

"Well, Beth, you silent now, after all I've done for you. Here comes miss slim waist and big you know what? And you dump me. Of all the rotten, dirty, dirty," said Melissa.

"Hold the adjectives," said Martha, laughing. "And dear girl, you haven't looked behind you recently, have you? Because that is the pot calling the kettle black." There is genuine laughter.

"Your tails know why you are here?" asked Bethanne. (Before Martha could answer her phone rings. Gabriel face pops up).

"Cuse me guys, gotta take this," said Martha.

"What is it?" Steph asks as she walks from the room.

"I know," said Sasha. "It's her godson. He's not calling me. My ego takes a beating so many times. He always wants to talk with Auntie Marty. I stopped competing years ago."

"So did I," said Keisha. "If Marty is around, I come in second. Look at that boy! Kiss her in public and I am not allowed to hug him. I can wave or pat his head or shoulder. After nine months, nine stitches and three hours of labor, no gratitude." The others laugh. Keisha very often changes the time and stitches for sympathy or emphasis.

"Listen, you two. That love was hard fought. Do you know the amount of baby food I ate back then? The amount of chewed up food they took from their tiny mouths and fed it to me. Do you know how many pieces of peach and ripe banana flavored with drinks I ate? Even with a straw they managed to leave gifts. Do you remember how they cried when I didn't drink? How they clapped when I was finished? You all run away, threw it in the garbage, hurt their feelings and I was left to pacify them. How about going to Auntie every time they made do. I did not buy it. I earned their love, so please go sit down and stop gripe," said Martha.

By this there is uproarious laughter. It is great that the comraderie is still alive among WASP. The family is in sync.

"Well, that's true. I don't know how you could eat what they chew up. Yuck. And I gave birth to him. Goodness, I used to wonder about that sometimes. You will roll on the floor with them. You were so happy to clean them. Plus, they never wanted anyone else to do it. After a while I just said boy it's not a prize or such a feeling dancing on the ceiling like Lionel Richie. Yes, I agree. You earned it, so much for biology! Gave up my girlish figure, stretch marks and get half saggy breasts. Little ingrate that he is," said Sasha.

"You were always so good with all the children. You organize birthday parties, and each year there was a theme. You should have a bunch of kids around you. You would be very happy," said Steph.

"I do. And have," said Martha.

"Where?" asked Steph (who has elected to use her middle name instead of Shaquana). Martha moves her head from left to right.

"I don't see any kids," Stephanie persisted.

Martha raises her eyebrows, her face reflecting amusement. When she said get it Martha pointed to all of them. The others laugh at Stephanie when finally, she understands Martha. She, too, joins in the laughter. The doorbell rings and the pizza are here. There is iced tea, guava and Martinelli sparkling cider, Martha pours half cider and half iced tea. It is so good. After the meal, they discuss and debate the pros and the cons and start date and frequency. Martha veto's monthly and they settled for biweekly Bible study. She is pleased with the outcome, and they settle for discussion about a family outing. Martha wonders if Great Adventures would hold the same attraction as years before. They talk about the Guggenheim Museum or Madame Tussaud's Wax Museum. She remembered when she saw Michael

Jackson and wondered at the details. She knew Madame Tussaud's got a gift. She saw Samuel L Jackson also. She was a fan. Maybe she'd take her children. They don't have to come. They debated seeing Purlie Victorious, The Demon Barber of Fleet Street and Here We Are. They decide the three names will go in a bag, thoroughly shaken then pulled.

"You guys are something else. Really. You're gonna do this? I think you are all reverting to your teenage years," said Keisha.

"No, girl. This is proper and professional. This here bag is an equal opportunity company, Equality people!" said Bethanne unrepentantly.

Amid the laughter Steph picks the show, they'd see Purlie Victorious.

"I am paying for my two children and me. Others are on their own," said Martha.

"Surprise, surprise," said Sasha. "I thought I was your best roommate. We signed a pact and now you throw me over for two scrawny delinquents. Where is justice? Don't know why I complain I never win. My best roommate. My best roommate," she said with make believe sob.

"I know, said Keisha. We can write a musical. You shouldn't dump me. You shouldn't dump me for two scrawny teenagers. Where is justice? Where is the justice?" she said.

"Gone to Marty everyone. Oh, when will you ever learn or when will you ever learn," sang Sasha.

Martha and the others applaud, and Sasha and Keisha curtsy and bow.

Keisha grabs a pen. "And the Tony goes to Keisha Burns."

"I want to thank God, my parents and my agent for getting this much deserved role. I am humbled in getting this award because of the strong competition. Thank you, fellow nominees, for being such gracious losers and for being not so good enough so that I can secure the win."

By then, everyone is laughing. At her impromptu mocking speech accepting her Tony Award.

"Who made your dress Key? Who is the lucky designer? "

"Oh, it is Christian or something," she said airily.

"Don't you think the back is too low for the mother of a teenage boy?" asked Bethanne.

"Know Bethanne you are old before you are young. My dress is designed by an upcoming designer who won Project Runaway. Girl I'm steaming – too hot to handle."

"Of course, you remember I dated Prince Harry. Dumped him, wasn't my type," said Keisha.

"Before you guys send yourselves to hell, let's see what is on tv," said Martha.

"Spoil sport!" said Keisha. "Or we could play charades. What am I doing?" (as she mimics playing the saxophone).

"Playing the saxophone, trumpet," said Sasha.

"Right. Who am I playing as?"

"Miles, Dizzy or Kenny G," said Bethanne.

Keisha is having a good time. At every answer she shakes her head. "Give up?" she asked.

"Yes." they said in a chorus.

"All of the above," she said outrageously and collects a number of cushions for her outrage. "I am good, aren't I?"

"Sure, you are good at playing an ass of yourself," said Stephanie drily.

As the laughter dies down Martha grabs a small book, How To Stay Focused. The book is not doing anything for her as the vague uneasiness grows bolder. What is the matter now. She found Maya but was sent away. She just couldn't push her way in. What now Lord she asked. She closed her eyes and sees a vision of her mother's face. She calls her mother and gets a busy signal. Really on a cellphone? Is there a conference? All these images are vying for attention. She does not understand the mixed message- first Maya now her mother. Thinking of her mother, calls again but this time the land line. Calvin picks up with a cheerful:

"Hey sis. How are yah? Coming by for a long overdue visit?"

"Not right now but how are you my favorite little brother?"

"Your only brother is doing fine, breaking hearts left, right and center. Always leaving some weeping female disappointed and disillusioned because I am unwilling to give up bachelorhood. Mom is in the bathroom. I figure that is who you are looking for. So, what's doing, aren't you coming to visit you baby brother?"

"No Johnathan Calvin," she said smiling. "Is everyone okay. Mom, okay?"

"Well, she has been super busy since recently. She is making secret appointments and going quiet if you enter the room."

"These appointments. Are they medical in nature? Has she been complaining? looks peeky, limping, well, anything like that?" asked Martha.

"Slow down. Mom looks as healthy as the proverbial you know what. She just has that determined look; lips pursed. So, I do not think it's medical."

"You can't know that. Maybe she is psyching herself up for impending results, putting her best foot forward, so to speak. Please get her for me or tell her to call pronto once she gets out the bathroom," said Martha urgently.

"Cool it sis. It's not a real emergency. She was very happy when you came home. She seemed freer, younger. Her eyes lost their haunting look. Her eyes sparkled again, and her dimples were sparkling as well. She and dad were making gooey eyes at each other. Thus, illness is not a part of this. She seemed genuinely happy," said Jonathan.

"Okay, I hear you, but please get mom for me," said Martha. The feeling of vague uneasiness persists. Why does she feel as if something is wrong?

Minutes later, her mother called. "Marty. How are you? I am glad to hear you," said her mom.

"I am great, Mom. How about you? Anything I should know about health wise," Martha asked bluntly.

"I don't know what you mean. I am healthy, there are no medical issues that sleep can't cure. What are you getting at?"

"I am just asking, you would tell me if something was wrong, wouldn't you?" Martha persisted.

"What is all this? Is John telling you tales again? And why should it matter to you?"

"Mom, I am just concerned. Talking soft and getting quiet as someone enters the room is an indication of secrecy," said Martha.

"What if it is? You of all people would know about secrets and isolation. Why, If I didn't know better, I'd think you cared," said her mom.

Martha sighed. It's apparent her mother has not forgiven. She has been avoiding barbs and darts from her mother. She understands, she hurt her mother with her thoughtless, rash, immature actions. Nana forgave her, grandpa Chimes, Charlotte and dad. Her siblings are great, but her mother is a different matter. She decided way back when she came home, she would not fight with her mother. She needs to suck it up, as her younger self would say. She has to bite back every angry retort that rears its confrontational head.

"Okay, Mom. I am sorry. As long as you and dad are healthy, that's all that matters. I am not prying. She said brightly, are you and dad going on a date this weekend, she asked as she blinks rapidly to stem the rebuff.

Her mother's tone softens. "I am sorry, I shouldn't have snapped your head off. It's just hard, next to impossible to ignore the fact that I have two grandchildren I know nothing about; and never see and never got the chance to bounce them on my lap, to hug and kiss them, to hear grandma." She said, a catch in her voice. She clears her throat and continues. "That's why I did what I did," she said defiantly.

Martha swallowed twice. She couldn't speak for the lump in her throat and feeling of dread. She tries several times. Throat is working, but her voice box refuses to cooperate. She inhales and asks, "And what is that mother?"

"I have engaged the services of a lawyer and explained everything to him about your giving up the children for adoption as a minor; on my right as a grandmother to see and get to know my grandchildren sooner rather than later", she said, sounding a little less defiant.

Chapter 5

"Oh mom! What have you done. Oh! my Lord! Mom you shouldn't have. Oh! mother why, why. Couldn't you have talked to me first. If I hadn't called, would you have told me'?" Martha could feel the tears trickling down. She breaks into a sob.

"Well Marty you had your say seventeen years ago when you hid your pregnancy and then gave up my grandchildren. You took that decision from me all those years ago. The subterfuge stops now. I made up my mind and no one is gonna stop me. It's full steam ahead."

"Where is Dad? Is he on board this disastrous train that will only end in a wreck. Do you know what it will do to Peter. Oh mother, please don't. Let us talk this through. Don't go charging in like a bull in a China shop" she said. There will be lots of hurt and pain," she ended.

"I am sorry Marty but I can't oblige. The lawyer will engage a PI to scrutinize the adoption. He will uncover what is hidden because it is fraud Marty. You yourself said Peter was stolen. You never agreed to give Peter up. The P I will find that nurse, the one that helped that crooked doctor," said her mother.

"Mom please! she pleaded. Let's talk! Do not do this. I don't want Peter hurt. He does not deserve this. He is innocent. He will be hurt and may despise all of us" she said.

"Sorry Martha I am not changing my mind. I did not get the chance to protect you, but that doesn't mean I am inept. I am in fighting mode. Death will be my only deterrent," said her mother.

"You have never forgiven me have you mom. It is your right and privilege. Please let us talk. Remember the Bible said we should not render evil for evil. I have repented for the pride that drove me seventeen years ago. I regret it. And I am sorry I made such a mess for you, dad, gramps, Nana and Gram. How long do I have to pay for this," said Martha despondently.

"Martha it's not about you. It is doing what needs to be done," her mother said.

"Is it mother. Did you think about his father. What if Ogwin shows up? Did you think of that. What if all his family members show up. Are you prepared for that. What about Peter? How will this impact him. Then it will be revealed he is a twin. When will it end mother."

"I admit I did not think about the father but, let the chips fall where they may. I do not want to hurt the boy. He seems an intelligent young man. Also, kids are resilient. If not now, he will appreciate the truth later."

"Okay mother, but I am asking again can we talk before you go ahead with this suit. Just for clemency's sake or just the fact that you gave birth to me. I have not been the sterile child you wanted, but in the name of who you worship and pray to give me ten minutes. That is all I ask," pleaded Martha.

"Okay but not until tomorrow about 4 pm. All the ground work I have/he has put in I'm protecting everything until we get to court. Sorry to upset you. I have to do this Martha."

"Yes mother. I see you tomorrow at 4 pm," she said quietly completely numb.

What is happening. She is blindsided. She looks up and Sasha is standing beside her brows in furrows. She looks at Martha's distraught tear-streaked cheeks and hugs her speechlessly.

"What is it pumpkin?" Sasha asked

Sniffling Martha shakes her head. "Do you know the day I was charged with murder I thought that was a dark period in my life. I thought it was fate and I was being punished for the attempted abortion and hiding my pregnancy from my Nana because she actually asked me if I were pregnant, because she suspected I was. I would just end the call and not answer. I thought I paid for that when Peter was stolen but guess not," she said.

"You still did not answer," said Sasha.

"My mother has hired a lawyer and is going to court to file for visitation. She is exercising her rights as a grandparent. There is a P I working and unearthing all sorts of information. She's going after Esther, and spouse can't remember their name now. But no matter what I say, she says she has to do what she has to do. No one or nothing will change her mind. I gave her most of the information she has now about Peter that he was stolen etc. Can you imagine the chaos?"

"Oh, Marty I am so sorry. Can I help? You know I am here always. You are afraid for Peter aren't you.?"

"Yes, I am. What if he does not want to know. Can we damage him emotionally or mentally. What if he believes I was stalking him and family. That I was at that park to gain his confidence, then snatch him from the stability he has known for so many years."

"So, what are you going to do? Are you going to get an attorney or are you going to try and stop her effort."

"Frankly I do not know what to do or if there's anything to do. There's no reasoning with her and I might have to counter sue to stop her. If he's brought up in the church, then he may know the story of Moses that his mother had to make drastic decision to save his life. I know I am stretching it, but I did care for him for two years. I loved and nurtured him. That should count for something."

"No," said Sasha. That is a valid reason. If he doesn't know about Moses you get the opportunity to teach him. He will see what a great leader Moses was."

"But can I fight my mother? Is that even allowed to breach your thoughts. For all the sleepless nights of planning and orchestrating look what it got me. It's like my life is chasing me down and I can't get away. If only I'd had the courage to face my parents and wasn't so frightened to raise a child on my own, I'd have my two children with me and not one here and the other unknown. I never meant to hurt anyone, just to fix a problem I created and yet, look how many will be hurt."

"Marty, you don't have to have all the answers or make a decision. Does your mother have a court date. What is in that suit. Girlfriend don't beat yourself up. You were brave and strong. You held us together and led us when we were frightened teens. You offered inspiration and motivation to go and become career women. Look how relentless you were so I did not lose my scholarship. You took over my son; sometimes I feel he's more yours than mine. Don't sell yourself short. You were and are terrific. Don't forget WASP even though we can't tell anyone. You got pregnant early and that's not a crime. If that was the only crime the jails would be empty. Didn't you tell me once you start living for Christ the enemy will send dart. You get me to believe so don't' forget Christ is with you. Pray it out like you always tell us," Sasha said.

They hug each with tears in their eyes. "Thank you, my true best friend. You are an A student. I've taught you well," said Martha. Sasha is her best friend despite their physical appearance. They are 'the' classic ebony and ivory. It is amazing how they mirror each other. There's such a bond between them Fort Knox couldn't stampede. They clean their faces and join the others; and there was no need to say anything. The conversation is general until bedtime. Martha calls Nana. She then picks up her Bible and reads Ephesians 6. She acknowledges what a loaded chapter it is. She looks at verses one and two – obedience and honor to parents, putting on the armor of God and Christians engaged in spiritual warfare. She knows this is not a coincidence all forces are converging on her. She prayed earnestly for strength and courage against the devil and to be infused with the Holy Spirit.

Next morning Martha is calm. She still doesn't know the best course, but she hangs on to Ephesians 6. She is exercising faith and believing. There are numerous lessons. There are fiery darts but, feet are shod with the gospel of peace. She is to take the helmet of salvation and the sword of the spirit while being an ambassador for Jesus. Obedience to parents relates to obedience to God. And parents are responsible to teach children about God. Is she disobeying her parents now? She doesn't see it. She is mindful that, that's, the only commandment that comes with a promise although it says in Matthew 15 'honor' not obey. And what of parents not to provoke your children? They are responsibilities on both levels. She will go with Ephesians 6 to the meeting with her mother. Parents are bound to correct but not with harshness and pain. However, she will empty her thoughts and not pre-judge. She is taking with her spiritual strength and faith. Her thoughts turn to Maya. Such a beautiful girl. She senses she is in pain. It is as if Maya knows and has given up. Is it an illness the doctors can't cure. The great physician Jehovah Rapha can. She must find Maya again. She wonders briefly if the message to find Maya correlates rather than juxtapose to her mother filing a suit to be acknowledged as grandparents. One of her flaws is over-thinking. Two relatives, she knows are happy about this flaw is her godson, and nephew Charles.

A smile curves her lips as she thinks of her nephews. Gabriel looks just like his mother Sasha. The face is the same also the easy smile. Charles is the image of his father, Jason. She wonders if there was a test to take before becoming a parenting how many would pass. She snorts at her cynicism. That could never be. God made the right choice- opened to everyone. Think of the many scholars whose parents cannot read or write. Children are really gifts and if so the small voice whispers, why did you give up yours. Shush! she said. It is because some people can and some can't. What if someone gives those couples a chance. Adoption is perfectly okay. Who wouldn't own Steve Jobs after Apple's technological revolution with the computer and I phone. And Mandela, the symbol of freedom although it's not technically adoption but was raised by Chief Dalindyebo after his father died when he was twelve. A man who refused to seek revenge on those who imprisoned him on Robin Island. And ate with the man who spat on him during the Apartheid era. Yes, became the President of South Africa. And Simone Biles with that beautiful smile is adopted. She is the G.O.A.T of the gymnastic world. Isn't mankind adopted in the family of God as well, through Abraham? She ignored how terrified she felt when she thought of raising a child on her own.

Feeling satisfied with her thoughts she calls Nana. Nana said she would love to meet both children but not at the expense of anyone's happiness. She became aware of her daughter's actions two days ago. She believed mother and daughter must talk. She did not have the right to tell her so left it to her mother to tell her. She would not take sides because she understood Dorette's position. She Nana got to bounce her grandchildren on her knees. Great-grand was a rarity but, she asked Marty to try and see it her mother's way. She digests Nana's words; let it sink in. Honestly, she wonders if unburdening herself about the children was her way of asking someone to do what her mom is doing. This thought stops her, and she sits up. Is her subconscious directing her steps. But aren't you supposed to when starting new, turning over a new leaf. Doesn't that entail cleaning the conscience and if it means confession then you do so. Well Nana agrees to be at the meeting, as a precaution.

Reluctantly Nana accompanies her though they arrive separately. Conversation is stilted but no outward hostility.

"Marty this is not to hurt you. I strongly believe you were under duress, that, the adoption was fraudulent, there was no legal representation, no counseling by the adoption agency, nothing. My lawyer will attack the process from that handle. Dr. what his name was a crook. He bartered babies. That is illegal. My daughter, she walks to Martha, I do love you. As a mother I feel I should protect you. I didn't seventeen years ago, and I am seeking to do so now. It's my job, my duty, my responsibility. Let me be mother."

As they both cry Martha could see the disruption in the children's life; the long-drawn-out process of breaking the seal, a litany of witnesses from the hospital to Esther and Johnathan Dunston. Will they be prosecuted. Did they know Gabriel/Peter was stolen? Is there a statute of limitation anywhere. What of the other children with the Dunstons? And Martha cried. This is all her fault. This is too high a price for disobedience. For the first time she wonders if she would be better off in prison. She found Jesus there so would be okay. Yes, maybe she would have been better off.

She realizes she is feeling sorry for herself. Is this the darts of the enemy that she needs the armor of God to prevent negative thoughts and assignation. As Martha leaves, she hugs Nana and Dad and her mother.

Her father whispers, "sorry pumpkin I have to stand with mom."

She holds him close fully understanding. She expects no less from him. 'No worries, Dad', the hug said.

"Mom, take good care of yourself. I love you," said Martha.

She makes one request to get a private hearing/ closed hearing with no leak to the media. In less than one week the lawyer from Dawkins and Haughton will present his petition to Judge Luther Marshall.

"I will try Martha. Understand I am not doing this to hurt you but, let me be a mother. I do for and behalf of my children, she said. It's when we hesitate, dissect over think things and rationalize, the particular situation becomes burdensome, then what needs to be confronted becomes the Himalayas if not Everest."

"Mother I was incarcerated what hope was there. What child wants that for a history- a convicted felon. It suited me back then; they did not know me. But once I had revived hope that I could get a second trial; that I would be released I made plans to tell Peter. That's why I went back to the park. I have plans mother, to let my son know who I am. I want to reestablish a bond with him but, if it doesn't happen that way, I already make provision for that through- never mind. But I want the opportunity to face him, tell him myself. I have to think, does he have to know the parents that reared him engaged in a crime. Do I want to do that. Will he thank me or hate me for breaking up his world. Yes, I over think situations, but it is never on my behalf. I am still learning to let God direct. Is Peter equipped for this? So, you see my desire to protect is innate. I have to connect with him outside of court. I can only pray for a miracle mom because I believe I worship a God of second chances. You see mom we are not fighting. I am not pitting you against your mother or your husband. I bear no ill-feeling there. The situation is being worked out Exodus 14 and 2 Chronicles: the battle is not yours but Gods. I am standing on that promise. I go to find my son. God bless you all," she said.

Chapter 6

Martha is surprised at the calm that settles over her. She does not know where she got the strength to make that declaration but she believes it. She is not fretting and, she is telling God what a marvelous consolation and she begins to sing, He's Got the Whole World in His Hands: Amazing from tumult to peace. God knows her heart. She harbors no malice towards Esther and Johnathan. Years ago, she read of obsessive females who are mother driven, who believe they must have a child and, would steal, rob or even kill. On the other side is, hysterical pregnancy with all the manifestations of pregnancy without a baby. She has an appointment at the park tomorrow. She is hopeful, Peter Dunston aka Gabriel will be there. She will seek to get in his head so to speak. She finds Every Praise on You Tube and plugs in her earphones and settles in a corner seat on the B train. She is undecided whether to change for the F or just walk home from W4th or visit the park there. That's an area WASP frequented back in the days. Maybe she can watch the guys shoot hoops in their 3 on 3 basketball game, then she'll go home and talk with Sasha, Natasha. She smiles at the pet's name.

It should really be Tasha and not Sasha. She chides herself, is that the big revelation- Sasha should be Tasha. She laughs at her own folly. Walking in W4th park there's everything to see. There are so many people milling around homeless, joggers' students' loafers, everyone.

Martha remembers how she believed Harlem was not in the city, that it was some place out there. She did not understand what Harlem Renaissance was. She heard her father talk about it and grappled to understand. It's ironic they taught $14^{th\ Century}$ Renaissance (way back in Italy) but no room for Harlem. Anyway, she loves to hear about Harlem in the 1930-1960. She remembered also Sue Simmons of NBC doing a look back. Her father was a musician. There was a picture of him with a bass guitar or something and a Caucasian lady somewhere who turned out to be her parents. Later a very young Sue was shown with big braids. She saw her in person, and she was slim with beautiful skin and was struck by how much she looked like her aunt Norma.

What's all this nostalgic outing Martha wonders. She walked the cobbled stones, turned on 5th Avenue and went home. Martha makes the sign of the cross as she enters the building. Maybe a vigorous shower would inspire her. There was a lot said earlier- all bottled up emotions. She has to be honest. Let down or betrayal seems to be on her shoulders. One thing is sure she cannot ask for forgiveness forever or continue apologizing either. She is tired of the guilt. Maybe it would be better if she moved away and give her family, really, her parents time to heal. It was naïve to think everything would be normal between them. There was too much water under the bridge. Now is reality time She will have to learn to keep her distance and lower her expectations where reunion and family is concerned. She adjusts the water to cold and full blast. The sprays stung and goose bumps covered her body. So much for an invigorating shower. It cools her body but not her mind. She decides to put the evening out of her mind and, rummages through her clothes to see if she has enough to enter the work force. WASP gave her clothes when she came home and now looks with a critical eye. One thing she remembers, a blazer is a must and pencil skirts preferably and numerous blouses. She is not in the mood to go shopping anyway. The doorbell rings and Charles and Gabriel are there, beaming. They both kiss her as they saunter in the room.

"What's up Auntie Em. Are you alone?"

"Yes. Why?" asked Martha.

"Because we thought we heard voices."

"I was talking to myself. I am looking at the clothes I have for work and deciding what is appropriate or not. Well maybe I said it out loud."

"That's okay Auntie. We thought you had a visitor."

Martha is intrigued. "What are you two up to and why the third degree?"

"Nothing said Gabriel. We notice how the men whistle when you walk by, and some nod and smile and look at you three or four times. So, Charles and I talked it over and agree it's okay if you wanna date."

Martha burst out laughing. "Oh my, my! How generous of you two. Thank you for your permission."

The boys look self-conscious but, Charles burst out: It's really okay if the ones that nod and smile who seem well, polite should ask you out and you accept for it's alright. We would just check him out."

He got a jab in the side from Gabriel for the last remark. Martha could not stop laughing.

"Who is she?" she asked Gabriel and then Charles.

"Who is who?" asked Gabriel.

"All this concern for my social life is flattering but it's not all about me is it. Some young lady, or ladies catch your eyes and you want to date her/ them. So, it is okay if you want to date. As long as I meet them, check them out and they are nice, by all means go."

"Oh Godmother! You know few women are as gorgeous as you are. We are proud to be your escorts. However, we can offer chaperone service or be your bodyguard."

"You don't have anything better to do," she asked.

They look at each other and answer simultaneously, "No."

Martha laughs and kisses them both telling them, "Now get out of here and tell your mothers where you are going." She shakes her head. Children! What a joy and a she cuts her thoughts still smiling.

You should always speak life in your children – Positive, powerful and uplifting. She loves the boys as her own. This part of her world she understands is comfortable with, the other part not so much. It's time to address the elephant in her thoughts. She will call Charlotte and ask her advice, then seek other legal representation. She is not about to cause friction between her father and his niece or the Chimes Clan especially the delicate Grandma Gertrude.

She talks with Charlotte and at once she finds out she can file an injunction against her mother to prevent the visitation. She does not believe it is going to be easy. Given all she has done and what has happened it takes chutzpah. She is aware too that filing an injunction can backfire but Peter (her Gabriel) is almost an adult and in a year or so is free to decide if he wants to know his bio-mother. On the other hand, she's afraid for Maya even more. She has no idea why she feels that way. She wished her mother had talked to her, discussed it with her before engaging a lawyer and filing for visitation. Her mother has no idea the can of worms she opened up. Why is she so opposed to this. Is she just punishing herself. She has major regrets about the adoption; has never made a secret of it but, for the unscrupulous Dr. Gruniche, she'd never have gone through with the adoption. She has always liked twins. There is something extraordinary about twins and she used to dream she had a boy and a girl. Welcome dream into reality! This whole scenario can only see disruption, discord and despair. Is she projecting her own insecurity. The lawyer Carlton Perry is very enthusiastic and thinks he can get even a temporary injunction. The Judge is almost certain to order an investigation. This is to protect the wellbeing of the child and to see if the child can be harmed by this issue. The children are almost 18 years old. Martha and Attorney Perry could not delay. She gave an altered version of the adoption, no counseling arranged by Sisters of Mercy and neither by Dr. Gruniche, her wayward teenage years, the theft of Peter. He said it is not going to be easy but, he is all in.

Martha remembered Mr. Perry's face when she told him about the case. If it wasn't so serious it would've been funny. His eyes literally bulged. At that point she was glad he got the short version. He seemed competent but what was most distressing, the day of the hearing was the day she should start working at NYU. In addition, she learnt she had to be there. Nana called told her that a gentleman from the court stopped by and she told her to direct him to W12th Street.

She got the subpoena and is overcome with fear. She reads it several times to make sense of it. The Respondents are Esther and Johnathan. Now she will have to tell WASP. She talks with Sasha. She calls Esther and Johnathan and leaves a message on voice mail. After a while she thinks maybe it is good they did not return the call. When dinner is over and the boys are otherwise engaged, she tells WASP about the court case. Steph asked her to start at the beginning. She obliged.

She told her parents, siblings and grandparents about her pregnancy with twins unknown to her at the time. The baby girl Sarai that was adopted but her brother, was stolen. Though in a haze realized there was a second child and Dr. Gruniche stole him and told her the baby was still born. She traced the baby and was his sitter for two years. Her mother wants visitation and files a petition. She made contact with him the day she met them in the park. She tells of taking Nana, and her parents and introduced them. Armed with that information her mother hired a lawyer. There's disagreement but she's determined not to fight with her mom. There's a request for private hearing to protect both children. No information can be told/ released to any type of media outlet. The flip side is she filed an injunction to stop this action by her mother.

"Marty I am so very sorry. That must be hard to go against your parents. How is everyone taking it?"

"Anything we can do to help? We got you pumpkin. You'll be alright," said Bethanne.

The girl group huddles around and hugs each other.

"We will pray her through this, right guys," Sasha comforted.

"Right," said Martha. "You know my go to Psalm-121 'I will up my eyes to the hills'; and Isaiah 41:10 'Fear not I am with thee'. Get out your phones and we will read, first the Psalm then Isaiah. They sit in a circle, and each reads a verse then the last two together and Martha Isaiah. Each WASP offers prayer for peace, protection, understanding, strength, patience and gentleness. Martha's prayer is longer and more in depth and went like this: Loving God, Maker of all mankind. Thank you are a God that forgives and loves unconditionally. We ask for your blessings, unity, understanding, peace and temperance. Help me not to be bitter about circumstances I cannot change. You promised you would be with us so we should not fear; you also promise in Psalm 37: 4 To give us the desire of our hearts. I pray for a healthy resolution and may there be no animosity among the family. And God please protect the twins. We pray that through your power you heal hurt and broken people. We ask in Jesus' name. Amen.

After the prayers WASP sits in quiet contemplation. Several minutes elapsed and they hug each other before going home. Martha's chaperones hug and kiss her. She explains it's a long day and is having an early night. Martha goes to her apartment and finds The Goodness of God. 'Okay Cece sing to me,' she said inwardly. She falls asleep with the music. She had a dream she was in the park in Westchester looking for Peter. There is an old man with grey beard and a cane who said, there is an answer. It is pink and white paper, and he walks off. In the dream she thought him strange and dismissed it. Next morning she has her devotion and later sings softly All Your Anxiety All Your Care. This calms her and she calls Nana. She is ambivalent, unsure if she wants to be there. She understands and is not upset with her. It's hard to see daughter and granddaughter on opposite sides. She wears a white sheath dress with black and plum stripes on either side and a concealed slit. Her makeup is understated but her face is flawless. She smiles and thinks Mary Kay should really start paying me. I really make their makeup look good. She grins at her reflection and leaves home.

She reaches Westchester Family Court at 9:40 am. She looks for Mr. Perry. He said he would be here on time and no later than 9:45am. Martha looked around. Where is her mother. She's unsure how this will be since it's private. Maybe she can ask the Court Officer. The hearing is in the annex- take the elevator at end of the hall and go one floor up and take the green elevator two floors down. Martha sees her mom immediately. Her hair was pulled back in a chignon, arched eyebrows, light eye shadow and Pink Wink lip gloss. Her mother is beautiful. She favors Mary Kay well. How strange some women do not want to be grandparents' afraid people will guess their age.

"Hi Mom. You look so beautiful." She moves towards and makes to kiss her, and her mother averts her head.

"Good morning, Dad." Face manicured and teeth gleaming as he smiles at her and embraces her.

"Good morning pumpkin. You look beautiful. You and your mom are easily the most beautiful women here," he said.

Where is the attorney, more so where are the Dunstons. What will happen when they see her. Will they be hostile and accusatory. Her lawyer comes in looking winded. He pulls her to the aside:

"I take it these are your parents. How are things between you?"

"We are civil," said Martha. I do not agree with their position. I am afraid it will disrupt the children, you know, their sense of being, a sense of who they are. Are they going to find Sarai also. I keep thinking of Pandora's box. But I give it to Jesus. He is much better at it than I can ever be," said Martha.

"Don't worry that is why I am here. Remember we filed the injunction. I reached out to the opposing counsel without success. However, we can't do anything about that now. Hon Douglas C Lee is the presiding Judge. He is fair and understanding and likes people to be punctual, and we are."

A court officer comes in to ask if all the parties are present. Her lawyer signs in. The Dunstons arrive shortly after with their lawyer. They looked terrified and it was obvious that Esther was crying. Johnathan is holding and squeezing her hand, Martha believes in assurance. The parties enter the court room and attorney Bruce identifies himself as attorney for Petitioner Dorette and Clifton Chimes; Samuel Bush attorney for Respondent Esther and Johnathan Dunstons and Carlton Perry for Martha Chimes. The Judge addresses the parties outlining the rules of the hearing. He understands the request for a private hearing and will grant that. His last question if there has been any attempt among the parties to resolve the matter.

Attorney Bruce explains the circumstances are different and unusual. She explains it involves closed adoption and an illegal adoption of a male child. Dorette and Clifton Chimes were unaware of the children until a couple months ago and would love to have a relationship with the children. They are asking that the adoption seal be broken, even if the adoption itself cannot be repealed, the grandparents want to meet and establish a relationship. The special circumstance is their daughter Martha Renee Chimes gave birth to twins, September 2004, a boy and a girl. Martha was 16 years at the time and left home. She would call periodically to say she was fine but never revealed her pregnancy. She gave the baby up for adoption.

During the earlier stage of pregnancy, she had no prenatal care and later when she went to the home for unwed mothers covering physicians withheld from her, she was carrying twins. So, she agreed to the adoption for one child. At the delivery she found out about the baby boy. Through trickery, the baby boy was taken without consent. Therefore, because there was no consent given for the baby boy hence the petition for visitation.

"What? A little unusual, you said? That is an understatement. Let me get this straight. Judge Douglas C. Lee summarized what he heard then asked if they had proof. For the first time the Dunstons look at her fully. There is a look of surprise and confusion on their faces.

"Yes, your honor. We subpoenaed the biological mother," said Ms. Bruce.

Her lawyer spoke up. "Your honor my client was subpoenaed and, will testify if warranted but, an injunction was filed to stop the visitation process."

"Have you now," said the Judge. "Just what is going on here. Does no one communicate anymore?"

"My client, who is the mother, believes such action is disruptive, maybe hurtful, even detrimental to the children's wellbeing; in addition, cause resentment and affect them emotionally. She would wish they complete high school or wait until they are 18 years old when they can choose. It is unknown whether either child knows he is adopted."

"May I speak your honor," asked attorney Bruce. My clients believe the need for acquaintanceship is not unreasonable but overdue. She was not given the opportunity to meet them as babies, never consulted. The decision made to have the child adopted was made by a minor, who was never declared an emancipated minor. But for the passage of such agreement would be null and void and should be vacated even though the adoption was made final. At the very least, the seal should be broken on the adoption for the girl."

"Attorneys, there are several issues here. It is interesting that the mother filed an injunction against the parents. I will read both your petitions and return here at 1:00pm sharp."

Martha tells Mr. Perry she wants to speak with the Dunstons and he advises against it. It might send the wrong message and affect the outcome of the case; worst may affect her credibility if she testifies. She greets them and walked to speak with her parents. Her mother is cool towards her but she ignores this and talks with her dad ending, tell your wife I am not her enemy. But she has the right to choose who she talks with. Enjoy your lunch, Dad."

Martha walks away and all the attorneys and court officers turn to look. She moves to the elevator oblivious to the looks she gets. Her mind is on her two children. Peter aka Gabriel, so handsome and polite. She allows herself to have one more luxurious thought of him; that he will be happy she is his mother. In a perfect world that would be so. Her mind turns to her daughter Sarai. What does she look like. She instinctively knows she is a beautiful child. She is smiling but abruptly Maya's face imposes her vision. She checks her phone; there is no call or text. Her wandering takes her to the park. She is not hungry because it is barely 11:00am. She finds a shaded area and decides exactly the Doowop music. However, what is playing is not what she is looking for but pleasant. It speaks of fun and romance; just walking in the rain. What she should look out for is pigeon droppings. They do not discriminate. She remembers her friend getting a full roost of pigeons on her jacket, when the M15 was rerouted on 2nd Avenue without benefit of shelter. Martha smiles, pulls her out her earpiece and gets ready to listen to Doowop 50s. Her parents' influence of music is a legacy she loves and appreciates. They always take her back to the Barbeques of her childhood. Her father loves to dance with her mother. Inevitably a party ended all barbeques, 4th July and Memorial Day. They are deeply committed despite her dad's teasing her mother about her bottom.

She listens to Doowop humming and singing the chorus. She is enjoying herself when her nose tells her she has company. She turns and sees a homeless man asking if she can spare some change. She told him she wasn't sure she had any change. She asked if there isn't a 'Y' near here. He shrugs and shuffles off. She never likes to open her purse to give money to anyone on the street. As he walks away, she takes two dollars from her purse. She calls to him: "Hey you are in luck. Here, get your coffee and bagel. God's peace."

It is a tragedy to be homeless. She wonders what happened to him. She regrets giving him only two dollars. She should've given him enough for a meal, not just coffee. He seems happy with the little and hopes he finds the 'Y'. She switches gear and listens to Bridge Over Troubled Water, so very apt. As the song ends a well-dressed man comes in her line of vision. It is the gentleman from Prospect Park.

"Well, hello again. And how are you doing today. You look very beautiful," he said.

"Hello to you too. Are you following me or are you looking for a change for coffee. Because if you are looking coffee the homeless guy beat you to it. Gave him all my change,' said sadly.

He threw back his head and laughed. "No to both questions. Why do you live here?" Adrian Boone asked.

"No, I do not. I am here on business, but we resume at 1:00 pm. What's your excuse?"

He smiled teeth gleaming. "I am a marketing consultant."

She groaned and rolled her eyes. You are not into crypto currency whatever that is, are you?"

"How can you disdain something you don't know about?"

"My humble opinion- find it boring, don't see the sense for it. And may be that man who ran away with millions to the Bahamas and leave his partner girlfriend holding the proverbial bag is another point. And just so you know I know about snails and octopus but I will never eat it. Just saying."

His smile stretched even further. She sees he's actually grinning and shaking his head.

"Okay it is a stimulating conversation but, can I invite you to lunch. I know of a place not far from here that's very nice. It's barely noon so we'll get a head of the noon day rush," he said eyebrows raised.

Martha isn't that hungry but maybe a salad and some fruit juice maybe. He is looking at her expectantly and sees the conflict/hesitation and presses forward. "I can show you my driver's license if you like. I am quite respectable. It would be a pleasure and honor if you would share a meal with me. I saw you give the homeless man money, and one good deed deserves another," he said.

"Okay Adrian Boone. Thank you. I will accept but I pay my own way plus, I need to get back in forty-five minutes, deal? Your driver's license please!"

"I don't like the condition, but half a loaf is better than none. You even remember my name Martha Chimes. Here is my driver's license."

"Thank you. I feel so much safer," she said putting her hand over her heart. They both laugh.

"What were you listening?"

"Just listening to music – Doowop etc. I just finished listening Bridge Over Troubled Water by the originals."

"The originals? Oh, you mean Simon and Garfunkel. I prefer that one too. What do you know about Simon and Garfunkel as young as you are?"

"Well Methuselah I know Johann Strauss and Bach too! And if that's your subtle way of asking my age, don't," she said cheekily.

"You got me there. Well, I believe you would be into Micheal Jackson, Alicia Keys, Katy perry Selene Dion and Patti LaBell who has crossed over. I love Patti. She is a lady of courage and strength. She has had some hard knocks and is still going strong. She symbolizes this with song New Attitude. Guess it is a blessing."

Martha nods her agreement. She's a phenom, but my girl is Gladys Night. But honestly, I love them both. Those two ladies are great at what they do. I love Patti in Different World. She's positively outrageous as Chipmunk's Mama."

They laugh as they enter Lee Morgan's Restaurant. The place is quite delightful and once seated, Martha ordered the salad with pineapple juice. Adrian is impressed by her decisiveness. As she glances around, he is looking at her. She is quite beautiful but seems unaware of this. There are shadows in her eyes that can easily be masked by her lashes or if she smiles. He really wants to get to know her. Is this his opportunity for further acquaintanceship. High cheek bones, full eyes, cupid lips, her face is flawless. Suddenly she turns and sees him watching her.

"What?"

"I am just thinking how beautiful you are, but you seem unaware of it. You are not conceited. When I first saw you at Prospect Park, I didn't really get you. Seemed a bit tense and on edge and then you smiled. It was pure joy. I've never been so captivated by a woman before and haunted by a lady before."

"Seriously? And you are not bashful either. Thank you but the saying goes beauty in the eye of the beholder. I was on assignment. Question is what business are you into?"

"I am an investment consultant- I watch market trends, monitor stocks, bonds and thereby predict changes in the market. So, when people need investment advice, they come to my firm Lavaville Investment. Why?"

"Do you believe in God?"

"What!"

"I said if you believe in God; that there is a supreme being?"

"As a matter of fact, I do," he said cautiously.

"Okay then. You see I am a Christian, and I have been cautioned about talking to strangers especially men. However, I believe in sharing the good news of salvation. That is what I am about- spreading the good news God is alive and miracles still happen."

"It is hard to exercise your faith?" asked Adrian.

"Not really. What I am focused on is to engage my friends then branch out to the wider comm unity. But the way you live speaks volumes better than any sermon- one you do not have to write. I embrace that because one can preach and not be sincere but, your walk will always show. There are preachers for hire that has nothing in common in expanding God's kingdom. But let the wheat and weeds grow together. At harvest they are separated. However, pointing finger doesn't help anyone."

"Seems like you have given this a lot of thought."

I've not always been this aware or a tuned to the goodness of God or believing I need Him," said Martha.

"With all the distraction and wiles of the world how do you remain so immune," said Adrian.

"One day you'll find out or I'll tell you. Oops! I have to get back. Thank you for the invite and the company." (She almost adds and not embarrassed herself so long she hasn't been on a date).

"You are welcome. It was my pleasure. Can I see you again- not just bump into you. I mean a real date. We can start by exchanging phone numbers."

"I guess we can but, if you change your mind no hard feelings," she said.

They walk quickly to the courthouse and part company. Martha hurries to the elevator. She gets back at 12:55pm. The others are there, and she smiles encompassing them. While she was with Adrian she forgot about the case. Now it's time to confront the matter at hand.

As they enter the chamber the Judge invites the parties to sit. He expresses empathy for the grandparents but, once the adoptions are finalized it cannot be revoked and the seal broken only under extenuating circumstances. There are things to consider like the child in question, the adopted parents and any ruling outside the norm may set precedent that might have dire consequences. I have ambivalent feelings about this. In addition, there's the injunction to prohibit the visitation. I need to study this more in depth so I cannot make a ruling today."

"Your honor," said Patricia Bruce: "I would like to make an appeal."

"Appeal on what Ms. Bruce. I have not made a ruling yet," said Judge Lee.

"Your honor that came out wrong. There are indeed extenuating circumstances and once known it will help you to make a more informed decision for want of a better word. Please your honor it is critical you hear this. I would like the mother Martha Chimes to be questioned/ testify under oath your honor. Her testimony will clarify a lot," said Ms. Bruce.

"So, the person who filed the injunction testimony can help your case. This I have to see. Ms. Martha Chimes take the stand,' and waves to the stenographer to swear her in.

After the preliminary to state your name for the record Ms. Bruce made sure she earned her fee. The questions are skewed towards her client. The questions make her look irresponsible and vindictive. So, she asked the judge to let her speak without the attorneys' questions or he should question her for clarification or she pleads the fifth, relevant or irrelevant in this situation.

"Do you know I can hold you for contempt and put you in jail?" he said.

"Yes, your honor. And I have been there before and maybe that's where I belong, my own personal home. (As she said, 'No Marte don't say that' said her mother). By these tears are streaming down her cheeks and she brushed them impatiently. Just one more inappropriate comment, your honor. This is not Face book or Instagram so I am not looking likes. So, forget the disparage," she said looking at Attorney Pat Bruce.

"I can see why the request for private hearing. This is highly emotional. Okay Ms. Martha. Calm down and take your time, you testify as you request. I do not like that you say maybe you belong back in jail. Wrongful conviction is the lowest form of our judicial system.

Chapter 7

"What is your educational level and in what field", asked Judge Lee.

"I have a master's degree and a Registered Dietician," you honor.

"So, tell me about your children."

I named my son Gabriel Ethan. She recounts she got pregnant at sixteen, did not tell anyone and left home. She went to Sister of Mercy- home for unwed mothers. She agreed to put the baby up for adoption. Up to that time she had no prenatal care so unaware she was carrying twins. Dr. Gruniche knew but never told her so the adoption papers she signed was for one baby. The father didn't want the responsibility for a child. He wanted his career and I was terrified. I had difficult delivery but knew there were two babies. I heard that baby cry and I told the doctor so. When he couldn't convince me otherwise said the baby was still born and showed me a dead baby. She traced the baby back to Esther and Johnathan and that's how I was his babysitter for two years.

Meanwhile they didn't know why he clung to me so. But it was an opportunity to bond with my son. Several times I made to abscond with him, but I knew there'd be a national hunt for me, even though I knew it was my baby. He has the Chimes birth mark on his shoulder. You see I never gave him up for adoption. He was stolen/ taken without consent. We got the confession from Nurse Gretchen Whitmore but, there is no record because the office was burned and Dr. Gruniche is missing. I am trying to do the right. I want him to know I am his mother but not like this. I do not want to barge in and disrupt his life. Does anyone care or understand that I am doing what mothers do; protect their children.

She exits the chair. The court room is as quiet as a grave yard at dawn. Even the clock is silent. Everything is out there. Esther Dunston is weeping silently with her husband's arm around her. The Judge addresses the Dunstons as to

Their knowledge of their adopted son. They disavow knowledge that their baby was illegal and without consent of the mother. As Mr. Dunston said he knew Gruniche for a long time. After his wife's third miscarriage they decided on adoption to prevent anymore disappointment. Preventative measures were not successful she reacted to the copper and him to the condoms. They practiced withdrawal but hat wasn;t successful either. He went to Gruniche, paid him and later paid extra to move up on the list. When Esther's EDD was known Gruniche knew and he'd have a baby for them whatever the outcome. It was a coincidence that the doctor had a baby for them.

The Judge is flabbergasted at this point. I will need to take this case under advisement. This is involved and unusual and without precedent. One hand a legal adoption then a questionable at best adoption, a request for visitation by the maternal grandparents followed by an injunction against the visitation by the biomother to prevent disclosure to her son. So, I will order a Court Order Investigation by Administration for Children Services in the meantime he will ask for a special counsel to investigate Dr. Gruniche, starting with Nurse Gretchen, Sisters of Mercy and the staff of Westchester General Hospital. They will return in six weeks. He will seek to lift the seal on the legal adoption. There is a grave miscarriage of justice. However, children are his primary concern. In the meantime, the grandparents can see Peter but not without the presence of his mother. Meeting must be intentionally casual as before but, they cannot under any circumstances reveal who they are. The court is adjourned until July 7th.

Martha talks to her lawyer, and for the first time realizes that the adoption papers for Peter might not have been finalized.

"So, you don't have any loyalty to the alleged adopted parents. How plausible that you get a baby right there in the hospital the day after your child is still born. They must have known something was wrong," said Perry.

You are very worked up about this," Martha remarked. "Remember it is about Peter no one else. What if he ends up hating me? What if he doesn't want anything to do with me. What if he thinks I was using him when everything is revealed. What if there are repercussions for the Dunstons. I think about that. That's why I want to get to know him."

As they turn to leave the court building, she turns to wish her parents safe travels.

"Can we drop you off somewhere," her dad asked.

"No thanks Dad," she said and kiss his cheek.

"So, you are not kissing your mom?"

"No Dad. It's just one humiliation per day. I tried this morning. She averted her head. Mom, you can let me know when you want to set up a meeting in the park. I'm sure the Dunstons won't make a fuss about it. It is a court order."

"Glad you are so confident of the Dunstons and considerate too. How very nice," her mother said sarcastically.

Martha refuses to be baited. "Mom, I told you before I am not going to fight with you. We have different opinions on how to handle a sticky and delicate situation. Whatever you may think I love too, more than you or anyone can ever know. But I am not going to debate that either."

"It's because of your deception and selfishness why we are in this position. If you were not such a delinquent those children would not grow with strangers," her mother said. "I never gave you away."

"Still haven't forgiven me yet huh? Well maybe it's too soon. Do you know Mom, I love you so much and all I ever wanted to do was to please you; to be just like you but, maybe it's just as well. Have a good night, Momma. I still love you." And her mother's words reverberate in her head. That was the worst barb yet.

And with that she walks away. She catches up with the Dunstons.

"Mr. and Mrs. Dunston I am.' but Esther interrupted.

"We don't want to talk with you. You deceived us. You knew who the baby was and then pretended you liked us. Go away, leave us be. We will talk when needed," said Esther.

"Honey, take it easy. She was hurt too. And she could've run away with him like she said."

"It's okay Johnathan. My mom sprang this on me too. I didn't agree that is why I filed the injunction, but I guess I am the fall guy for everyone. You get home safe."

She walks off shaking her head. It is about 2:30pm, the train must be empty now and she heads towards the station. What a day! Well Martha, you certainly have two parties mad at you. You are on a roll. Lord, keep me in your care; watch over me I pray she says inwardly. Just as she is about to enter the station her phone vibrates. The number is unfamiliar, so she ignores it. It is a good reminder to turn the volume up. The phone rings again and she ignores it. If it rings again, I will ask him to send a text. She is in deep contemplation as she rides home. The day has good points and not so good points. She remembers Adrian and smiles, handsome to boot. That touch of gray by the temples, gleaming teeth undoubtedly eye popping. A smooth chocolate with an outrageously appealing smile. He is well manicured, and she likes that. He has good breath too and she chuckles. She could be interested, and bad breath is one of her pet peeves. Honestly, she doesn't like to see people with missing teeth either. She's amused each time she sees the commercial advertising dentures and the lady is without front teeth. She often wonders why the front teeth are decayed or missing.

She hops the 4 train and gets off at Union Square. She can go see a movie, stroll to the green market, just visit the stores or church on Park Ave. No that is too much walking plus, she doesn't have walking shoes. She'll just saunter up 14th Street to 5th Avenue. She can go to first Presbyterian or the Dutch Reform Church. Imagine First Presbyterian is over one hundred years. She loves the stain glass windows, but her favorite is the pipe organ. She remembered the first time she heard a pipe organ as a child it seems to be vibrating inside her and her body shook. It is like she is hearing it. It is so real she is gripped by emotions. She should see if they are rehearsing, then thought it is early and working people maybe on the choir too. But maybe the Music Director is warming up. She quickens her steps, worth a try.

She walks in and runs in a young seminarian. They talk for a while; she just returned to the neighborhood and visits there. She hoped the choir maybe rehearsing or Music Director would be tuning the organ. The choir rehearses Thursdays but Bible Study is Tuesday at 6:000 pm. She thanked him for the information. He tells her he is doing vocational training. He has his master's in divinity. He wants to be a pastor one day. He went to Colombia. They talk about theology and scriptures. She tells him she is undecided whether to pursue pastoral pursuits. They exchange phone numbers so they can discuss Bible issues. He is Disciples of Christ but interning with First Pres. Martha feels better and walk the half block home. As she enters the building the phone rings. The same number as the last two times. She picks up cautiously.

"This is Maya. Do you have time to talk?"

"Oh Maya! Gracious Dios. I am happy you are calling. You have been on my mind. Yes, baby I have time to talk. I just got home.

"Do you remember when you told me I had shadows in my eyes."

"Yes".

"Well, I do," said Maya with a laugh.

Martha sensed she is being jovial to keep from crying. "Where are you?"

"In the hospital," she said. I get to hang out with the old folks. Some are bald without teeth. Do you know I can't understand why people don't have teeth. Eek! Sort of gross me out. Anyway, I close my eyes not to look at them. There is a little lady with blue eyes and a pixie face so cute. She talks about FiFi her dog all day."

"Maya, what is wrong with you?' Martha asked, stifling her agitation.

"Well, it's like this. I have kidney disease, you see. I don't know if it is from urinary tract infection or from Ecoli bacteria. Two years I had trouble sleeping, fever and fatigue. So, they said it was chronic kidney disease (CKD). Said it could be reflux from the bladder obstruction that prevents blood from getting to them and whole lot that I can't remember or understand. What I know is I am stage 4 of CDK list which means the method used to measure the amount of blood being filtered by Glomerular filtration rate (GFR). So, my blood isn't being cleaned properly," she said on a sob.

"Maya I am sorry. I didn't know it was anything as severe as that. I do not know what I can do to help. But I will do anything that will help you.

"So, you see why you should have stayed away from me. But I will tell you something that will make you sit up. I only have one kidney," she said crying now.

"My darling. Where are you? I am coming now. Don't give up. There must be a way. God sent me to find you. That is no accident."

"I am at Lenox Hill Hospital in the city. I remember your face each time I close my eyes you come in my vision and I decided to call you."

"I am on my way Pumpkin, just as I am," said Martha. She hurries back to Union Square, takes the 4 train to the 6 train to 77th Street. In loafers, is able to move fast. She gets there in half an hour. She calls Maya and asks the floor and room. Martha is shocked. The name is the same as in the dream Maya Sturgeone. She takes the elevator to the third-floor room 332. Maya is there as beautiful as ever and for the first time she realizes she looks like her mother Dorette Chimes. With the head tie she is her mother's twin. OMG. Her eyes fill with tears. Is this what is called a God wink. She looked up and thanked the God of miracles. Is this her daughter. She must pull herself together. She looks so small against the pillow and the sheets up to her shoulders. She hugs Maya.

"My baby girl!" She sees the butterfly at her wrist and the drips hanging from the IV pole. She looks tired but smiles bravely.

"I am sorry you have to travel all this way to see me, but I remembered that you said anytime. I do not know what to do," said Maya.

"What do you mean. Where are your parents."

"My Dad came to visit until 2:00 pm. Mom will come 5:30 – 6:00 pm. I am doing dialysis now. Thankfully I took early finals in two classes. I have only four left. I don't think I did well on the last one, I was feeling too sick. Still, I may scrape through with a B based on my course work and midterm."

"That is great. So, finals are over. I know what that is like."

"Are you still at college?" asked Maya.

"Yes and no. I attend Colombia School of Divinity. I have not decided if I want to be a clergyman. It's exciting studying the scriptures, the social justice classes. It explains why Dr. King spoke so much about social justice and delving deep into the Bible seems God's cause is always directed towards justice, in the Old and New Testament. But I digress. There is still time for me to decide. But what is the treatment program for you."

"Kidney transplant is her best option or be on dialysis. I have been doing it at home for three years, that way no one knows. However, I was running a temperature, and it is part of periodic checkup but I think I have an infection from whence I know not. So here I am feeling sorry for myself, and I thought of you."

"Where are you on the kidney transplant list."

"I have been on it for three years. I got a number of calls and each time it seemed like a match then at the last minute something came up to make it not a match. So, I go back to wait."

The nurse comes in to take the temperature. Afterwards she said she has a temperature. She will have additional antibiotics and fruit juice. Maya asked for something exotic like Big Bamboo drink served at FDR Resort in Jamaica by the pool and bar together. The nurse said just as exotic she offers, apple juice and cranberry juice. With laughter trailing the nurse. Martha says she is glad she is not morose and asked if she believes in miracles.

"I used to, but I don't have the faith to believe any more. I do get morose at times but that has lifted since you came. I believe it was a long shot you showing up but then I said how could it hurt. So, I am happy to see you," Maya said.

"Would you believe Maya I was directed to find you? I had a dream three times the same thing to find Maya. I saw you in the dream slim and beautiful with shadows in your eyes. God directed me to find you. I asked what to do when I found you. I did nothing at first and the day I saw you physically I was finishing exam when this person said go find Maya in Prospect Park. I looked up and saw the back of the person. He was wearing ecru. I ran after him didn't see him and asked some students if they saw him, they said no and gave me strange looks. I said okay God it has to be you. I will find Maya and I found you."

"Are you kidding me?"

"No. I was sent to find you. How could I know your name. I asked you surname and almost passed out when you said Sturgeone. In my walk with God, I asked him to use me to further his kingdom. So maybe I am here to offer comfort so let us pray. Gracious God, maker of heaven and earth, we invite your presence. You said where two or three are gathered You will be there. Thank you for the life of Maya and we pray for her healing. Send us a word or a sign that your will, will be done. You promise to give us the desires of our hearts and what we desire is for Maya to get well. Send her a kidney God and this time let it be a perfect match. O great Jehovah Rapha, you great healer, hear our petition today. In Jesus name we ask. Amen."

"Thank you, Martha. I feel so much better. You know my grandma says God speaks to us but we don't listen and that he hears every sincere prayer. Many prayers have been said for me in the past but, this time I feel different. I feel renewed hope. I thank God, you gave me your number that day. Here you are sitting with me in the hospital. I cannot thank you enough."

"You are welcome, Maya. I told God I will serve Him. I've learnt so much about the Bible- its teaching and meanings. There are so many things I did not know about faith, believing and understand what God is able to do when we come to Him through Jesus. And I've learnt to ask. Ask and it shall be given to you, seek and you will find. As simple as that I found you. I feel it inside you will be alright. You will get your kidney. We just have to agree together. Do you believe you will get that kidney?"

"Yes, I believe. I feel so at peace. Can you stay with me until I fall asleep?" asked Maya.

"Of course, and she holds Maya's hands. Maya's eyelids flicker once and with a smile falls asleep. Martha watches and tears roll down her cheeks. This is my baby. I've found her. Thank you, God, for second chances. I can bring my daughter real comfort. She kisses her hand, then kisses her forehead. As she straightens, she sees the nurse watching her.

"She's a great kid isn't she," the nurse said.

"Yes, she is." Martha agrees. A terrific kid! Now all that is needed is a kidney. Martha turns to go and sees the lady coming towards her. She seems Hispanic or close enough. Martha nods and as they pass, the eyes look familiar. She looks back and she is going towards Maya's bed.

As she leaves the hospital she's deep in thought. She reasons the day I bear my soul in court, offered a contempt citation, she sees a child that could be her own. She felt drawn to her even in the dream and more so after meeting her. However, her mother is angry at her, likewise Esther. And her mother has a visit with Peter through her. So, there is balance. What are you teaching and showing me Lord. Do you want me to lay hands on her? How about I pray for her in privacy. Open my eyes to see you and my ears to hear you. I am too tired to think. Direct me how you want me to go. She goes in the subway and heads home. As her head crests the subway, she thinks she sees Adrian. She hurries after the figure afraid to call his name in case it is not him. The man meets a lady and they embrace passionately, and then she sees it is not Adrian. That reminds her she has to find out if he is married, or single and free to mingle as they used to say. No need to think about him. He hasn't called. She hurries home to her bodyguards. Of course they are waiting for her. Amid hugs and kisses they share their day. Martha goes to shower. She needs time to process the events of the day but, with her chaperones, has to satisfy them first. From earlier she had them hooked on Jepoardy and each time she hears Johnny Gilbert she expects to hear Alex Trebek.

There is lentil with smoked turkey. The slow cooker was her friend in the past and still is.

"Auntie where did you go today. You look like a model," said Gabriel.

"Well back in the day meaning a long time ago I used to model. I traveled to Jamaica, Bahamas, California and many other places. Those years I was very skinny. Now I am about twenty pounds heavier," she said smiling.

"Really/ You do not look it. You are still slim, right Charlie."

"Yeah. Is true. Would you model again," asked Charles.

"I do not think so. Maybe if I am tempted to do a shoot in Hawaii, Bali or Australia. Which reminds me I must get a new passport if I'm to leave the USA. Do you have passports?"

"We had when we were babies. We going somewhere?" asked Gabriel.

"No, not right now but, you never know. It is important to be ready for unexpected treats. Anyway, I am going to have an early night. By 8:00pm I should be in bed."

"Aw Auntie Marty, but why?" asked Gabriel.

"Because it was an emotionally draining day. I went to Westchester, came home only to rush back to Lenox Hill Hospital. There is a young girl that needs my help. Do you remember me telling you that God speaks to people, not just like in the Bible?"

"Did he speak to you Aunt Marty. What did he say. Did he sound like in the Ten Commandments," Gabriel asked eagerly.

"Do you remember how Mary and Joseph took Baby Jesus to Egypt to hide him from Herod?" asked Martha.

"Yes, in a dream. What did he say to you and were you afraid."

"Slow down Champ. I was not afraid. He said go find Maya. I had the same dream three times. The last time he spoke I had just finished my test, and he told me to go to Prospect Park and I will see her there. In the dream I saw her face so, I knew who to look for. I found her but she said she was alright. I knew she could not be because God knows everything. I asked her to take my number and if ever she needed me to call night or day. I got the call today. I believe God wants me to help her, but I don't know how. She is in hospital. She needs a kidney."

"So, Auntie Em, you are saying God knew she was going to be sick and need a confidant," said Charles.

"Yes! The dreams, the voice, all that specific information is not accidental. I even knew her name. She stops abruptly. No need to get maudlin. Want us to pray for Maya yes? Let's hold hands."

They prayed for restoration of health; for Maya's healing and grace and mercy. After they kissed goodnight. Martha does her nightly devotion and goes to bed.

She falls asleep but is restless. Her sleep is not straight and not uneventful. She's at the hospital, then she's in the park. One minute she can see, the next she can't see, but she is searching. Each time she walks towards the light, the darkness is blocking her way. Get thee behind me Satan, you have no power. Christ got the key to death, hell and the grave. And the darkness moved, and she was in an open field and a mountain range in the distance. The sky was never so blue, nor clouds so fluffy and white. Wow, God painted a masterful vista. There was a gentle breeze. And two small birds skimmed the air. And the majestic eagle soars. Rolling Plains! Blue capped hills and nearby the waters tinkled. She could not believe it and the mountains beckons and she walked towards them proud bastions in the sky and its surroundings. There was no path up, and she lifted her eyes and hands to the heavens.

She woke from her dream. She is half mad, half glad she's awake, but highly dissatisfied. What a scene. Where did that come from? It was so beautiful and tranquil. Maybe it's a place for the soul and mind to rest. It is only 5:00, not time to wake. She falls back into a dreamless sleep. This time she wakes about 6:30. She gives them 5 minutes before she wakes them. Even if school will be out in another two weeks, they should not be late. She wakes them up and they stumble around. They vetoed cooked breakfast and accepted cereal instead. She offers Cheerios.

"Oh, no auntie, that's for kids," said Charles.

"What about Bran. It has raisins."

"No auntie. That's for little old ladies with constipation," he said, laughing uproariously. Reluctantly, she joins in, shaking her head. As they finish eating, she reminds them to brush their teeth.

"Oh, Auntie Em. We just brushed when we got up," said Gabriel.

"Well, one, the milk will give you bad breath and two no kisses. Or at least gargle with Listerine.

"I'll take the gargle," said Gabriel.

"Me too." said Charles.

As they bond out the apartment, she tells them go tell their mothers good morning.

"Okay." they said in unison.

She knows them so well she does not close the door, and one pops his head in and kisses her a second time. They love and affection those two lavish on her is obscene. No wonder their mothers call them traitors. She has no idea how. That excessive love would play out in later weeks.

Now she is alone. She tries to digest yesterday at the hospital. Oh, my Lord. Is Maya my daughter? For all the weeks she agonizes, she does not know where her daughter is God was lining this up. It is so powerful. What's the probability of that happening? Now she is beginning to understand. When David pronounces God does awesome things for him. He knows the goodness of God. He says God's work and turns situation; the awareness of God's mercy, justice and bringing things to pass, making a mockery of our plans, showing up and showing out. She sinks to her knees and begins to pray. Thanks, God, for his mercy and intervention. She asks for Maya's life. Whatever is causing the kidney not to function, blockage, abnormality of its formation, result of meningitis, or Ecoli bacteria, whatever it is, to please save her daughter's life. She tells of her gratitude for keeping her in Bedford Hill and connecting with her children. Her maternal instincts are crying out. She wants to shout the goodness of God. She is bursting with excitement. She wants everyone to know. But can't right now.

She is sipping hibiscus tea when the phone rings. It is Adrian. Greetings over he asks if she is at work.

"No," she said without expanding.

"Do you have time for lunch with me? my treat."

She declines citing things to do.

"What about dinner then," he asked.

"It depends," she said.

"Depends on what he asked. Do you want to go out with me or not".

"I told you it depends. I need my day loose in case I have to leave at a moment's notice", she said.

"And dinner?"

"Well, it depends on where," she said.

"What is the matter. Is it age difference. I don't seem trustworthy. You saw me in daylight twice. I can understand caution that's why I suggested lunch," he said.

"Adrian it is not what you think. I live in Manhattan, that's why I say it depends where. I do have something on my mind but, evening is good,' she said.

"Just to make you comfortable and feel secure, choose a restaurant you like," he said easily.

She is tempted to tell him Wolfgang but tells him Drayton Restaurant on E12th or Maestro on 8th.

"And what time do I pick you up?"

"About 6:30. With luck we can get there by 7:00."

And what's the address Ms. Chimes."

"It's 71B w12th Street EE01 between 5th and 6th Street."

"I know where. That is, it's my old stomping ground when I was a lad. You make mischief in other people's neighborhood, not your own. See you later, my dear." He was gone.

He does not understand her plight and she has no intention of telling him, even if he has pretty teeth. She likes him, but it's not the best time. She has not been on date in how long? She has not had interest in men in a long time. With the exception of the Warden, there was nothing to look at, at Bedford Hill. And since she's been out, no one like Nana would say nothing that full eyes. Now here's an idea she will call Nana. Nana asked how things went the day before, she told her, she testified, and the judge said he'd decide under advisement. Granted decree for her mother to visit, but not without her, and cannot disclose the relationship. They go back in July.

"Nana, do you know how you are always telling me God moves in mysterious ways, that sometimes your secret longings are made manifest after you sort of give up. Well, something happened yesterday that is wonderful. I met someone unexpectedly. It makes me so happy, it's like finally, the burden on my back fell off. I have been giving God thanks and claiming the victory."

"I am glad Pumpkin; you used to be happy. Is he a nice person, someone your Nana would like? Nice manners as well as nice face and brings home a paycheck."

"There you go, Nana's way ahead." Martha realizes Nana believes she's talking about a man. Oh, well maybe it's better that way.

"So, when is Nana meeting this gentleman?

"Oh, Nana, behave, it's too soon. I met him in Brooklyn, then I saw him in Westchester yesterday and we shared the table."

"What you mean by that?" asked Nana suspiciously. Mean he too poor to buy you a meal? That no good son of a"

"Stop, Grandma. You have it all wrong. We met in Brooklyn and yesterday when the judge adjourned the case he invited me to lunch. I didn't want to because he wanted to pay for it. I agreed to go if I could pay for my own. He agreed because it was half a loaf. We talked for a long time. He called today and invited me to lunch today, but I have other plans. He invited me to dinner. I accept and he will pick me up. 6:30. Satisfied now?"

"Now that sounds better. He's not taking you to some cheap eats, is he? Where you have to hold your bag in front of you and look two sides of the road." By this time, they are both laughing hard.

"No Nana, I know the restaurant. I gave him the name of the restaurant. It's fine dining."

"What are you going to have?"

"Nana, it's morning now. I don't know, I'll see what my palette calls for and it's not Dutch. He is paying."

"Good girl." Nana said.

"Know, Nana, you are too much."

"Girl, you are not getting any younger. You need a companion, someone to exchange thoughts with, to grow old together. It was a sad day when your grandpa passed, but we had almost five good years and forty marvelous years. Never regretted it one-bit marrying Robert. He was all I need and Jesus. It was complete."

"Yes, Grandma, both you and daughter Dorette married the right partner, so that is what I want too. If not, I'd rather do it by myself. He doesn't have to be perfect, just sincere, honest and very loving. Anyway, I believe God will give the desires of the heart. When there's something to tell, I promise you, Nana, you will be the first to know. I have to go dress for my appointment. Love you, Nana."

"Love you, pumpkin."

Martha gets to the hospital. There's a tall gentleman by the bed. She hesitates briefly, then walks towards Maya.

"Good morning, Maya. Good morning," and turns to the gentleman.

"Good morning, Martha. This is my dad, DC Pierce."

"Nice to meet you," said Martha. Mr. Pierce's eyes are assessing or trying to remember her. Martha's heart throbs in her chest and she said, "I will return later after your visit with your daughter.

"Who is she?" her father asked.

"She's a friend. We met in Prospect Park.

Martha hurries out of earshot. Now that she sees how much Martha looks like her mother, would anyone else put two and two together? Oh dear. She walks outside. She walks towards ambulatory surgery and goes in. She feels safe. She is hiding. Martha, you are a coward, she chided herself and answered back; a happy one too. I'm not about to confront that man. He may remember me from the adoption. He may misconstrue my being here. Besides what if he makes a scene or worse gets her banned from visiting Maya. Oh no. A happy coward indeed! She starts reading the book of Esther. She needs courage. She reads for an hour and sees the room is almost empty. She makes her way back to Maya. She is alone and Martha is happy. Maya looks pale and listless but smiles once she sees Martha.

"I was afraid you wouldn't come back, she said. I like it when you are here, it makes me feel better. It's like God is watching over me. Not that you are God, but that's what it feels like. Anyway, you said God directed you to me, I believe that. Right now, I am feeling more hopeful and more energetic.

"God is always with us; He is not busy. You know the Bible says he writes the names in his hands. That's Isaiah 49 verse 16. So, he knows you, me, everyone. That really got me going the first time I saw that. It means we are important to him. He thinks about us all the time. That is why we should never be alone or lonely. The Bible is a fascinating book. It teaches you; how to live, how to love, how to serve, how to be redeemed and how to get salvation and how to have faith and believe in Jesus; the one who paid for our sins. I get real excited reading the Bible. It's like what's next?"

As she stops speaking, Maya looks at her with shining eyes. "Your face lights up when you speak. It's like, not you. It's a glow. I can see you are passionate about what you believe. I believe God sent you to help me because suddenly I feel much healthier. Does that make sense?" said Maya.

"Yes Maya, the presence of God energizes us. We feel light the fact that a burden is shared. If you go alone on a dark road, you feel afraid but if you have company, you will feel better. You don't feel alone anymore."

"Why do you think I pushed you away in the park? And ever since I started feeling sick, I saw you in my mind, even in my sleep. It was only when I got to the hospital that I had the courage to call you. It was a compulsion. That's why I think my getting well is tied to you. I'm not an ardent Christian, but I do believe in a capital God, I don't think this world came by accident. There are too many phenomenal things. There's so much order in nature; that's why I do not have a tremendous amount of friends outside of school. I am weird."

"Maya. You are not weird; thank the Lord you can think. You have insight grown folks don't see or know. Nature is its own palette. It will usually correct itself. But we are not good custodians of the earth, and we have destroyed most of the ecosystem. We have destroyed the ozone layer. The glaciers are melting. Sea level used to rise one inch every century but, global warming changed all that. And the human brain who can fathom? No, you are a thinking, breathing intellectual, one of God's prized possessions. You are beautiful and wonderfully made," said Martha, kissing her cheek.

"Thank you. I know we'd get along the first day we met," she said, laughing.

"Of course you did," said Martha, sharing a real moment of camaraderie with Maya.

"You are cheery today," Maya, said the nurse and looking better too. Your temperature is normal."

"Did my blood work show reason for my temperature, and my output."

"No, but you will need to speak with your doctor." She looks at Martha as she said that.

Martha stays with Maya until after lunch. "Okay, dumpling, you look better, so I'll leave you to your nurse, she said hugging and kissing her.

On the way-out Maya's nurse stops her and asks to follow her. "Do you know Maya's father?" she asked.

"No. Why?" Martha asked.

"Today he asked about you. He said he didn't want you to visit Maya. I asked why, he said he just didn't want you visiting his daughter."

"I don't know why. That is strange. I met Maya. She seemed so delicate but had shadows in her eyes. It was divine for me to reach out to her, and so I did. Is it written somewhere?"

"No, and I just forgot he comes in mornings. I believe you are good for her. She changed after your visit, and I saw her a while ago. Everything is better, including her spirit. And since I don't know you, we never talked."

On impulse, Martha hugs her. "Thank you," she whispered. Nurse Johnson may turn out to be another nurse Radcliffe, the one that aided her in tracking Peter down. 'Man appoints and God disappoints.' She will continue to see Maya. Thanks for Nurse Johnson's tip. So maybe DC Pierce did recognize her. Doesn't he know a mother's instinct to care protect their children? What does he know; he's only a man she laughs. Well DC you must be English because DC means district constable. Therefore, you snoop and pry, which under the right circumstances is good, but not when trying to mess with God's work. She cheers herself up as she walks to the 77th St. subway. She looks around to see if she sees DC or if anyone is watching her. She is careful to keep her dark glasses on. Now she knows she has to resume aspects of WASP Fashion and mannerism. As she nears home, she begins to flip through her wardrobe. What can she wear tonight? Spandex, suit, no and spaghetti straps definitely not. She'll wear slacks either white or cream, with a black or navy blouse. These combinations flatter her looks and she wants Adrian to know he's dating the best. Oh, no. Belatedly, she remembered her bodyguards. Oops. That may be awkward. She'll just remind them they said she could date.

Her date? Was one to remember. It started when she told Gabriel and Charles, she has a date that night. They want to know the name and where he's from; where he works, where they are going? And when she would be home. They are peeved she did not tell them earlier. She explains He called after they left for school. They did tell her she could date and what a good idea it was and still is.

"Well, we have to see him and talk with him, you know, man to man, right, Charles?"

"That's right, we can't let you go off with a stranger without meeting him and getting a picture of him, to check him out," said Charles.

In addition to Gabriel and Charles the WASP knew; they added their two cents. When Adrian arrives Gabriel and Charles meet him at the door and introduce themselves. We want a word with you later, said Charles as Martha comes from the bedroom.

"Hi Adrian, did you meet my nephews?"

"Bodyguards, Auntie," said Gabriel.

"Yes, as a matter of fact I have," said Adrian.

"Why are you guys dressed up. Thought you are going over by Gerald's for pizza night."

"Yes, we were, said Charles. But change of plans, we have duty tonight."

"Really, what duty is that, Charles?" Martha asked.

"Bodyguard duty." They chorused. Martha's lips twitched.

"Okay boys, no need to change plans. I do not need your help tonight. It's your day off. Night off."

"No, can't do, Auntie. We will accompany you and your date. It's as simple as that," said Charles.

"You cannot come. Adrian is quite capable of taking care of me. See he is big and strong."

"That there is a problem too. He doesn't look like a pixie, and we will be there if he gets out of hand.

"Okay boys, the game is over. We have reservations and we are going by Chelsea," said Martha. Excuse me. She goes outside to speak with Keisha and Sasha. She explains her dilemma and they say they are not involved.

"Come on guys, we have reservations. I do not want us to be late," said Martha.

"We are not keeping you. You have two boys you spoil rotten who forget we are their parents when you are around."

"Seriously. You gonna do nothing? asked Martha. As she walks away.

"You look fantastic though. We'll come see the great Adrian who coaxed that date out of you," said Keisha.

"Don't do me any favors," said Martha.

Keisha and Sasha are right on Martha's heel. They introduced themselves.

"We just wanted to see who could tempt my best friend on a date," said Sasha.

"Not that bad one honey. Couldn't have done better myself. Okay sis, go have fun."

"Fun. Fun. What kind of fun?" asked Charles.

"Okay, Gabriel and Charles. I have a date with Adrian Boone and we are going to dinner. You are causing a scene and if you don't stay away from my dinner date tonight, I will personally skin you. Do I make myself clear? Bodyguard or no bodyguard, you are off duty.

Kiss, kiss," she said. The boys kiss each cheek. "As for you two delinquents, we talk later."

Sasha and Keisha are unrepentant. "That's what you get for spoiling those boys. See, Mr. Adrian, they ignore us if Auntie Marty is around. Listens only to Auntie Marty. She goes on the street, they escort her. One on either side. So, they belong to her. Simple!"

Martha walks out and toss over her shoulders. "Go to Gerald, don't disappoint him." She turns to Adrian. "I am so sorry for all that. I saw them give the I am watching you sign."

"No, it's fine when two young bucks would rather be with their aunt than their own buddies. It speaks a lot about your relationship. Oh, I almost forgot you look gorgeous. So, I do forgive your bodyguards," he said, laughing.

"Bet you have never had such an experience before, being confronted by two teenagers ready to do battle for" Martha is cut off.

"Their beautiful aunt. Not bad. It's a worthwhile experience. I showed them my driver's license for them to validate," he laughed.

"How embarrassing. They are on punishment," said Martha with feeling.

"Don't worry about it, I have handled complex situations before," he said lightly.

He sees Martha biting and gnawing at her lips and said consolingly.

"Their hearts are in the right place. I too am smitten by Auntie Marty. So, on behalf of the smitten, I beg for clemency for one Gabriel and Charles and Adrian," he said. And casually brushed her lips with his.

She laughs. "Well, this time, but only because you ask so nicely. Coupled with the compliment, I hereby grant clemency as requested."

They pull up outside Maestra restaurant because it is early. They find parking pretty near the entrance. They walk in silence and enter. Quickly they are seated. The hum of conversation is all around and she looks around to see if there is anyone she knows. She notices that the diners three tables away are staring at them. She believes they are staring at Adrian because he is handsome in a dinner jacket; beard and moustache expertly trimmed invariably will draw attention. She ignores the looks and Adrian orders pre dinner drinks. Later she orders her favorite grilled salmon, asparagus, carrots and half a roasted sweet potato. He orders well done steak with potatoes and vegetable medley. The food is delicious, and they eat with enjoyment. Just as they finished this gentleman comes to the table. He seems affable enough, laughing and shaking Adrian's hand.

Oh, Adrian. Didn't know you are back on the market man. Good to see you. And who is this lovely lady? he said.

Adrian feels obligated to introduce her." Walter Henriquez, Martha Chimes.

Martha takes his hand and smiles. "Pleased to meet you."

"The pleasure is definitely mine, although you seem familiar somehow.

Martha smiles and shakes her head. "You sly old fox, Adrian. We have to get together soon. The sooner the better, old man. We certainly missed you," said Walter.

"No, you don't. You are saying it to be polite. Anyway Walter, good to see you. Best regards to the family. And take care," said Adrian easily.

"Why do I get the feeling you are not happy to see Walter.

"Truthfully, not really. Tonight is new and fresh. I do not want leftovers, and that's what Walt represents to me right now," he said, smiling. "There is an upside to this, you know."

"And what is that? Martha asked.

"I finished eating. No chance of raining on my appetite," he said with a grin.

Martha laughs. "Ouch! That bad, huh?"

"What do you want for dessert? Key lime pie, pecan pie, German chocolate, Junior's Cheesecake and ice cream, what's your pleasure?

"Wow, quite the spread, but maybe I should pass because since I came back from- I have gained about ten pounds in the last two months. My grandma is an excellent cook and baker and, I've been packing on the calories.

"Oh, you can afford to eat a slice of something without dire consequences. The pies are great and pistachio ice cream. Umm, you want to eat it?

"I get the feeling whatever you eat. Slides off you like butter on hot spoon back. Me not so lucky. It shows all over," she laughs.

"Come on. Tell you what. We share a slice of cake and a small scoop of ice cream. Well, what do you say? he said. Please."

"Alright. Share a slice, but you have to choose the ice cream I like deal."

"Deal. So, it's pecan pie and what ice cream? Let me see pistachio, black cherry or grape nut."

"Well, I'm glad you changed your mind. I almost didn't get any ice cream. You are an ice cream fiend."

"Thank you, he said, laughing. I thought you were watching calories."

"Because of my generous nature, I decided to save you and throw caution to the wind and eat the ice cream for you. Therefore, you should be thanking me."

Adrian laughs clapping his hands. "You are unique and utterly amazing. Thank you. That's very generous of you, Miss Chimes."

"Tell me, isn't that going to build on you, eating all that ice cream?"

"No, she said. It's for a worthy cause. The calories are held at bay as compensation for the cause". They both laugh, drawing the attention of diners to their left and right. He asked if she is under curfew.

"Since it's barely after 9 o'clock I can stay out a while longer. What do you have in mind?

"We can drive down to Chelsea Pier as it's only a short hop from here we can stroll and see if Orion is out.

"Orion, eh?"

The path is lighted and because it runs along Hudson River Pkwy, they walk along this tree lined path. Because it's balmy the pier is crowded, but they move along freely, looking at the water, boats and lights. After about half an hour the pier got a lot more crowded. And then they leave. As they approach her building, a car pulls out immediately in front the building. He immediately pulls in beaming. As they approached the front door, he holds out his hand for the key. He opens the door and steps back. She thanked him, telling him no need to accompany her to her door.

"Oh, no, no, no. That's not how I roll, as the kids say; pick you up at your door, I drop you at your door. They reached the door and before he could put the key in the lock, it swings open. There are the two boys.

"Thank you so much Mr. for bringing Auntie Em home safely and before 11:00.

Martha raises her eyebrows in exasperation, trying very hard not to snap at them. She glances at Adrian, biting back a smile.

"Thank you for a lovely evening". He hugs her, kisses her cheek and whispers. "Next time we dump the bodyguards."

"Oh, right Uh-huh, she said. And goodnight. It was a pleasure."

"The feeling is mutual, he said. Goodnight BG," and runs down the stairs.

Listen, young men, we have to talk now. I understand you want to look out for me. But that's not your responsibility. I am an adult and I can take care of myself. The situation could have been very awkward and embarrassing. Luckily, Adrian has a sense of humor. Do not pull this stunt again."

"Oh, Auntie, you don't know how you look." said Charles.

"Oh, Auntie you just don't only look good. You are fine, really fine. There are animals out there. Some men are really animals. They don't know how to act. And we are here to protect you. Remember you have not been on a date for a while," said Gabriel.

Martha couldn't help herself. She laughed loud and hard. "I don't know what to do with you two. But seriously your job is not me. See about your education and college. Enjoy the upcoming weeks before you get serious with college. Got that?"

"Yes, Auntie. So how was your date? Was he a gentleman? If he wasn't, we'll straighten him out, said Gabriel. See these?" showing his biceps.

"Thanks, but go to bed. The jealous pair may be waiting for me to say goodnight so, get to bed you two and see you in the morning. I might have to go to the hospital to see a friend."

Martha sends a text to Maya asking if she is being discharged. Maya replied maybe we'll know by 11:00 AM. Martha puts on a cyclist pant and sneakers and jogs to the park, circling Park Ave. South and walked through the market at Union Square. She start up E 17th St. so she'd go to 7th Ave. and back home, that should take care of the extra calories, despite her boast to Adrian. As she stopped for traffic on 6th Ave. she sees Walt hat's his face. She's hoping he would pass her, but no such luck.

"Hi there. See you twice in 24 hours. Where is your companion."

"Hi there. Who?" Martha said.

"Come don't be coy, Adrian of course," said Walt?

Martha is praying for the light to change as she is running on the spot. "Honestly, I don't know, home I guess," said Martha.

"You know, I couldn't place you last night. But know, you looked familiar. You are the one cleared of manslaughter, or was it murder against that? Judge what's his name? Saw you on The View or was it GMA? You are a sly one. Many hens have tried after that rooster and you swoop in. Does Adrian know about you?"

"Wish I could stay and chat. But I have the light. Bye." And she took off like mercury. It is to be expected since she was on TV a couple of times. Now she is wondering if that was the right move. What the heck, it's in the past, can't change it. She turns on 7th Ave and jogs to 12th and enters her building. She will shower, do her devotion and wait on Maya. She will leave and get there when the dad is not there. There is a complication she does not need. Maya called and asked if she could be there after her dialysis treatment. Treatment is for three hours- from 8 till 11. Martha replies by text promising to be there. Briefly, it crosses her mind whether the father may be there given the dialysis. Well, she'll get there about 11:30. Just in case she'll text/ call her before she enters the ward as a precaution.

She showers, has a smoothie, and does her devotion, after which she checks the volume on her phone as well as for any missed calls while she showered. There are two missed calls from Dad and Adrian. She returns the call to her dad first.

"Hey Daddy, how are you doing? How is mom? Everything okay with the bunch?"

He laughs, "slow down Pumpkin, I'm fine, Mummy's fine, everyone is fine. How are you? I was asking your sister if she spoke with you and she said no."

"I'm fine Dad. I've just been busy since Monday. Do you believe in divine intervention? Something happened on Monday that led me to believe that. What? That aside, when does Mom want to meet with Gabriel aka Peter? I need ample time to set this up the first time. I want and agree with it to seem like happenstance, and by all means it should.

"What are you talking about, Marty?"

The judge said meet but don't disclose relationship right. So that's why the first encounter should look like chance meeting and not arranged. I have to think of what they will tell him. What if he knows and refuses to visit with us? He is almost 18 years old. And I want him on our side. I am praying for a smooth seamless transition when the time comes. See dad, before mom's precipitous actions I was working to get him to trust me. All that day, you were all there, I was cultivating a relationship. Trust is essential, Dad. We need his trust but if she tries for Memorial Day when many people would be at the park or any other day, I will arrange it. You know that it's almost the end of the semester, they may have half days, remember. I have his number, although I will set nothing up without the Dunstons being aware."

"Ah Pumpkin! I wish there was not the discord in the family. Just when I thought our circle was complete with you coming home, now this. Both of you have valid points. And stubborn like no tomorrow, he said wearily. The other children are trying to be neutral, but it is hard."

"Dad. I am not asking anyone to take sides. If they have a side should keep it to themselves. Remember I'm not looking likes. I am neither Facebook nor Instagram. I didn't give much understanding seventeen years ago and it's coming back at me, so I'm not fighting. But I will have to contact Ogwin and his mother and sister at least. This is part of my predicament. I need time to set things in place and now I am thrust into a situation, so it goes to show we all make errors/mistakes. Tell them to be cool. I'm good. I'd never ask anyone to take side with me or expect it. Gods got this. He is working It out for me. He will show me where and how to go.

"Okay honey, but why are you so Busy."

"I have a friend that's hospitalized and needs my help. I feel this is an opportunity to make a difference. And I will. Pops, don't worry. God Forgives sins. Love you dad."

"You too, Marty," said her father.

She is about to call Adrian and remembers Walt. Oh, no! What if he called Adrian and blabbed? Well, there is one way to find out. And she calls him. She will not mention Walt.

"Hey, gorgeous. Happy you called and you didn't leave me hanging," he said.

"No, I would not do that. How are you?"

"I am better for hearing you. Do you think you can ditch the BGs? They are worse than Dobermans."

Martha laughs. "I hope you never tell them that because it will be worse."

"Worst. How come?" asked Adrian.

"You don't know. They'd be so proud of themselves, a real feather in their cap. They'd start putting together all sorts of notion of how effective they are as BGs. I would be in torment. It would amount to house arrest because they will not accompany me on dates." she laughs. "Don't ever say anything like that."

"Thanks for the tip. So can you ditch them?"

"Maybe. I will see when they are visiting the grandparents and my girl pals meet weekly. Maybe this Saturday is movie night, and I could ask for a rain check for that."

"Okay, Saturday. It is casual, pick up. at 4:00 pm, if you are sure the BG won't be there."

"Tell you what I will tether them so you will not see them. Anyway, I will let you know if the coast is clear. There are six of us who have been friends for almost twenty years. If a date can't come to the house, someone will be followed. He is deemed untrustworthy. So now you know."

Adrian laughs. "Well, you are pals, but it's good you look out for each other."

"One day I'll assemble all and you meet them. You met two, the jealous pair. Anyway, talk later. I have an appointment. Stay safe."

The ride to the hospital is uneventful. She hesitates before entering and finds an alcove near the administration office and sits. She needs a kidney. Martha jumps. And he looked around. No, she must be imagining things. She needs your kidney. What? she exclaims, jumping up. She sees two staff members in scrubs look at her strangely and one asks if she is alright. She said yes but they continue to eye her. Okay, mind now that you have people thinking I am a lunatic suppose we have a talk. What are you talking about? After a minute of silence, she said. And now you are silent. Martha is so distracted, forgets to call Maya to see if the coast is clear. She hurries in and her eyes are listless but smiles.

"I thought you weren't coming. Dialysis wears you out, but I know if I see you, I will feel better."

"Well, here I am. Martha holds her hand. The hands are soft. And you can go to sleep because I know you are tired. You say you will be going home. Where is that?"

"My home is really in Westchester, but I stay with grandparents in Brooklyn. It is easier to get to school, but not the whole truth. My parents are separated."

"Oh, I am sorry. Are they thinking of reconciliation?" said Martha.

"At first, they were, then they are not. Both my parents refused to talk with me about what was going on. For more than two years they have been apart, so I stay with grandmother most of the time. We had a fight, and I threatened to leave home but went to grandma. I refused to live with either of them. Do you believe God will heal me, Martha, she asked.

"Yes, darling He will, keep believing and praying," she said.

Maya falls asleep and Martha watches the rise and fall of her chest. She seems so vulnerable the more she looks at her, the more she looks like her mom as she sits and watches her sleep. The earlier conversation with her mind rushes back. Me give a kidney? The last time someone took a scalpel or forceps to me all but butchered me. I escaped by the grace of God. Go back their Lord, let it be something else. I still feel the forceps. Tearing into me and whatever other gadgets they were using in that dimly lit dingy room and the quack as he -She stops tears streaming. Oh God. I cannot do this. I do not have the strength, she cries, as if her heart is breaking. A hand jerks her up.

"What are you doing here? I left orders. You are not to visit my daughter, said DC Sturgeon.

Martha is totally floored but eventually finds her voice. "Take your hands off me," she said in a cold voice. She has ice in her veins and she's a cobra ready to strike. Whatever he's about to say died. The look on her face stops him. He drops her arm. She is bristling and says calmly.

"Maya needs me. I am here for Maya, not you or anyone else. I will visit her morning, noon or night. One in the morning. noon, 4:00 pm, whenever I choose," said Martha. Every word offered with emphasis, conviction, and an even tone. DC is a tough man, but he has never seen this in anyone more so a woman. Quickly, aggressively defensive, look so deadly he knows who she is. And if science is right, the Mama bear is the deadliest opponent.

"I know who you are. You cannot do this," he stutters.

"Maya called me. That's why I am here. I am Martha to her, a friend. I am not here to hurt you or your wife, but I have something I need to do." She said, knowing it's reasonable to be upset. Belatedly, she wipes her cheeks. "Are you going be here when she wakes up? Then please explain to her for me why I left." She walks away without looking back.

Martha has to compose herself. She is terrified of having surgery. She doesn't mind really giving up her kidney just the methodology. She prays there's a match found soon for Maya. She breaks into cold sweat just thinking about it. Maya is discharged later that day and expresses disappointment Martha was not there when she woke up but understands she was uncomfortable around her dad. Son of a gun, so he lied his way out of that. They promised to call daily and when necessary. Martha realizes Maya is lonely. She encourages her to call even one of her school pals, but she seems reluctant. She has two favorite cousins Philip and Kalia. Martha encourages her to keep in touch, not to hang with someone old enough to be her mother.

Maya declares, "then who else should I hang with? They say parents and children should be close, right?"

"You are absolutely right. I do not want to invade your family's privacy," said Martha.

"It will be okay with grandma and grandpa. That's my mother's parents. I am their favorite. I want you to visit," she insisted.

"I will on condition I speak with them first. They must offer the invitation. Plus, we can facetime. It's better than nothing, but I am glad you think of me as a friend and a mother figure," she said softly.

Chapter 8

It was two weeks ago they had the hearing. Trying to guess when her mom would be available was trying. She did not get angry with her or raise her voice. In the end she called the Dunstons and asked if Memorial Day weekend would work for them or the following week. They chose the following week. Martha called her mother and gave her the date. Her mother was angry at not being consulted.

"Mother, she said patiently. I called three times, and each time was a different issue; in the bathroom, you have to check your schedule, so I chose a date. You have time to make any adjustment, but grandpa and grandma Chimes along with Nana I'm sure would be happy to go in your place, right? Now that's an idea. Later. Bye mom. Let me call them."

Martha hangs up the phone. Two minutes later her dad called. She explained her efforts to tie her mother down for a date. Finally, she went ahead and set up a meeting. Mom said she was not consulted so I told her I'd invite Grandpa and Grandma Chimes and Nana.

"You did what? Martha Renee Chimes!"

"I called three times, Dad. It's the Saturday after Memorial Day in the park, said Martha. Now it's up to her to show up or not. I am not in a fighting mood, just want peace. The weekend when many were leaving the city, she had a picnic in Central Park with Adrian, WASP met him and were charged. He bumped fist with the BGs telling them to keep up the good work. Pride showed in their faces. They were offered an invitation to share the picnic, which they politely declined. Sasha was going to see her parents, which meant Gabriel would too. Keisha would visit cousins in Long Island. Steph and the others would be home. Adrian surprised her with his culinary skills, but she was sure he had help. He said he started cooking very early that morning. She enjoyed the corn on the cob even though. There was no elegant way to get the kernel husk from under your teeth, except picking it, well, she politely turned her back and did so. There was sparkling cider, lemonade and grape juice with lots of ice and fish kebab, and kebab, shrimp, lamb, fish and chicken. She teased him asking if he expected company. He said her BGs might have crashed the picnic. They listened to music. It was obvious he liked The Drifters, Percy, Sledge, Four Tops, Temptations, Dion, and Jay and the Americans, Dionne Warwick, Gladys Knight, and Roger Whittaker. Martha used to listen with her dad, so she was comfortable. He commented she wasn't old enough to know all of them, but she told him of her dad's preference. It was pleasant, and relaxing. She found out he lived on the Upper East Side and wasn't surprised based on what Walter implied.

Her relationship with Maya continued to flourish. They spend a lot of time on camera. Meanwhile, Martha contemplates her foray in the ministry. She continues to see Adrian for supper, lunch, dinner, dessert, whatever he comes up with. The unease about donating the kidney never left her and she prayed for courage to obey. She gets up the nerve to tell Sasha about her fear and what God lay on her heart. Sasha is consoling, not to overthink the situation and let her faith guide her. She would be available to accompany her anytime. Now she is afraid to go to sleep because of what she may dream. With fear and trembling, she contacts Lenox Hill Hospital and Maya's doctor. When he hears of a possible donor, he calls her. They set up a screening as the meeting with Peter looms big and difficult.

She says nothing to her parents, especially since the meeting was awkward and the conversation stilted. For the most part, once her brother Jonathan got there, Martha introduced him, telling Peter what a pain he was. Jonathan retaliated that she was mean to him.

"Well, I am surprised you survived, Evileen young man, you were lucky. I should have hidden your sneakers.

Peter visibly relaxed after the banter." My mom could tell you stories of John's escapades, right, mom?"

Mother said. "Yes, he tried to sneak out to a party. He slid out the window and dropped right in my arms. He did not know what to do with himself. I had his father's belt. One lash and he climbed the wall like Spiderman."

As they all laughed, Jonathan said, "well I was cured for a long time after that and to add insult to injury, I was grounded for a month and had to do, everybody's chores. I raked leaves, washed dishes, washed clothes and worse, had to clean and wash the bathrooms. Thus ended my life as a swinger."

"That is why we called him Spiderman," said Denise. I know my sister brags how super you were as a baby, but did you do anything outrageous?"

"Not really, I loved sports so one day I went to MSG for a Colgate meet. My parents could not find me. I was punished. No class trips and no TV for a week. Grounded for two weeks and no phone. I became acquainted with Crayola and coloring books. That's how I became a stickman genius. Oh yes, I also learned how to hold a conversation with myself. Luckily my punishment ran concurrently so I took the pain one time."

After that they snacked, the boys went to shoot hoops for a bit. When they returned everyone ate. As they ate, Martha watched Peter smiling. He looked up and saw her watching him.

"What?" he asked.

She explained she keeps seeing Baby Peter, so chubby, cute and loving. How the other mothers and babysitters envied her. He did not cry a lot although he loved to run, fell a lot but he didn't go far. "You were such a joy to me. You were never tired, and I never needed a gym. I chased you enough. You were my buddy though."

"You still seem to see the baby and not the teenager. I'm still cute and cuddly. If not, I'll grow on you. Seriously!"

"Is that so. We will hold you to that. Unless some girl told you that. If so, tell them they need my approval"

They played games and after hugging everyone, Peter left. She walked with him to the edge of the park, hugged him and kissed him and wished him good night. As she returned there it was quiet. She asked what the problem was. Said she should have made more effort to engage Peter with the family. She asked how; she is open to suggestions. She reiterated she did not support this move to ambush Peter and she did what was required of her. Furthermore, she had other things on her mind. She assisted Nana with clearing away the containers and other stuff used.

"Marty, honey, when is this going to end?" asked Nana.

"I don't know what you are talking about," said Martha.

"This back and forth with you and your mother being at loggerheads, I mean," said Nana."

"Nana is it because you all still regard me as a child that I must do what the parents want/say. I cannot believe because I have different a point of view, I am automatically wrong and reduced to being a child who is disobeying her parents. I am an adult Nana and for those who don't know, I stopped being 16 a while back," said Martha.

Martha collects the debris and heads for the trash.

"Well, I'm off folks, get home safely and godspeed parents, siblings, and Nana."

"Marty, wait up. Don't you want me to drop you somewhere?" Jonathan asked.

"No, my love, it is Saturday, and you can get caught in traffic most foul. But thanks. Love you," she hugs him. "Love you too big sis. He's a great kid, I can't imagine the courage it took to walk away and the pain of not telling him you are his mother. Don't worry Marty, everything will work out. You are not a mean person."

"Thank you, John, you are the best. So wise beyond your years," said Martha. Martha heads for the train. She is not mean; she wants what is best for Peter. She had plans to tell him when she was sure he trusted her, so he'd accept her and not turn tail and run. Anyway, she has more pressing issue Maya, she started the testing for compatibility. The 24-hour urine test, blood test, Electrocardiogram, lung test and the tissue testing, she wonders if these are preliminary tests and she did all that, what is the point? Oh, three months. She cannot understand why the process is so long. She is agitated and wonders why. Is it precipitated by guilt because she was reluctant due to her fear of surgery? In two more weeks, they go back to court, and she has this dread. Maya is going to what? Lord quietens my heart and still my fears. She mutters, Isaiah 41:10, Do not fear, I am with you. Then she says a prayer for thanksgiving for finding her daughter.

The day of the hearing, she is very nervous. The attorney said he is sure it will not be decided as there are too many issues, possibly fraud, kidnapping, fraud, collusion, felony and a host of other legal issues. The persistent ringing of her phone shows Maya calling, asking her to come see her.

"I am at an appointment, and I'll be there immediately after," said Martha. She is upset by the call because Maya. knows of the appointment. Another fifteen minutes and she call, and Maya doesn't answer. She finds it strange. They enter the judge's chamber and her phone starts ringing it is Maya.

"Maya," she says as she bolts for the door.

"Maya is sick and we are taking her to the hospital," said Mary.

"Oh my gosh no. Where are you? I'll be there pronto." She returned to the hearing.

The Judge stated unfortunately, he did not make a final decision because of the criminal element involved in the case. The findings on this case had to be turned over to the DA. What he will say in two weeks Sisters of Mercy staff, with Westchester General Hospital staff will be here to testify as to ascertain Miss Chimes did give birth to twins. There must be evidence somewhere. At that time, Nurse Gretchen Whitmore will testify as well. Visitation continues as previously ordered.

Marha rushes from the chamber with a hurried greeting for her parents. Maya needs her when she gets to Lenox Hill Hospital. She heads for the ER. She doesn't see Maya, but her grandmother, Mary Andrews.

"How is she? Is it her kidneys?" asked Martha.

"No dear, something she ate and it's some form of bug coupled with indigestion. She was writhing in pain, sweating and dizzy, I jumped to a false conclusion. Sorry to get you upset and running like that," said Mary.

"That's quite alright, I would have done the same thing." she smiles at Mary.

"Her doctor, Dr. Osmond, came to see her. Once he knew she was in the ER, that made me feel a lot better," said Mary. Martha squeezes her hand. "Do you know, I feel Maya is going to get well and be a normal teenager. She has suffered from this ailment for so long and it's quite a trooper," said Mary. Martha nods in agreement.

"Yes. She is a remarkable child. How much do you will believe in miracles and that God talks to you?" she asked Mary.

"I believe miracles are all around. You and I, being here is a miracle. God moves, and he changes, and he shifts because his will must be done. We miss our chance of being excellent when we disobey, but God has His way of getting us where we should be. Think Jonah- didn't get very far did he. He got a body full of fish smell for his running away. Can you imagine the smell, she said laughing. God will have His way."

Martha hopes fervently she is not 'a Jonah". Look how God worked it out that she finds her daughter. That request was in her heart, yet God has sent her to find the Maya. Oh God, how excellent is your name in all the earth pops into thoughts. Yes, she said. A whole lot of fish smell.

"Do you know someone implies the book of Jonah is really about man's conscience, but I am not so sure. There are too many lessons to be learnt. Learning to forgive and don't throw stones is invaluable for man's survival."

"That is right so is obedience. As the Good Book says, obedience is better than sacrifice," said Mary.

"Do you know this world is getting smaller every day? Imagine less than a month ago I did not know you, but here we are, united and bonded in love for one little girl. Our God is awesome. I feel it too. Maya will get her chance to be a normal teenager and dance if she wants to, go on hikes. It is a glorious day, Mary," she said softly.

Think doctor orders clear liquids, unsweetened juice and water to flush her system. The doctor has to walk a tightrope between giving or not giving antibiotics because of her kidney disease. He orders she is to be held for three hours for observation then she can go home.

"I had a hard time convincing my daughter not to leave work and I'm glad I did. I must call her."

What a difference. She has no one to call. She thinks of Sasha and Adrian. This she will share with Sasha tonight. There are still times Adrian is watching her, when they are together. It's as if he's waiting, wanting to ask something. He lives easy, but she feels there is more than meets the eye. For one she can't understand why he is still single and he's getting on in age and so are you, said the inner voice. And who asked you? she counters. You know, my situation was different back in Bedford Hills. The pickings were slim, less than none, so she has reason. She will ask him the next time they meet. He's attentive, polite and quite amiable. But she senses distance too. He had accompanied her to First Presbyterian Church, and she reciprocated by going to Marble Collegiate, Doctor Peel and Arthur Caliendo's, old Church. It's so tranquil looking but, it's the heart of those who worship there is the issue. Martha decided years ago not to be overly concerned about that. That's God's work. She has to be reflective of his love, caring and compassion.

Martha is brought back to the present when a voice said, "what is she doing here?"

Martha slowly looks to see the father. Okay she's thinking. Let Mary answer.

"My DC, glad to see you but why so short? said Mary a frown on her face, "I called Martha."

"Oh, where is Maya? Is she alright?" Martha does not respond. She looks at her phone as the best way not to deal with DC Sturgeone. Mary answers and Martha closes her eyes. Thankfully now all she has to do is tune out his voice and have communion with God. Truly, He is Jehovah Jireh. The situation with DC and the way he is behaving it's like spreading the table before her enemies. Is it instinct? Or he knows she's Maya's bio mother. The last evidence is yet to be revealed. Maya is discharge ready and Mary turns to Martha and thanks her for coming, promising one day to speak about the scriptures. She kisses Maya's forehead and whispers, love your pumpkin,' nods to DC, hugs Mary and leaves. Martha walks away. DC's eyes narrow and Mary asked if he knows her and why he is unfriendly towards her. She has been a friend to Maya, who said she reached out to Martha, and she came. DC has no answer, so he said guess he was taking her for someone else. As Martha enters the subway, she is unaware of being watched. Her mind is on the court case. If all of those people testify, she needs to sit with the lawyer. He has to mount a defense for her. She calls Perry and apologizes for rushing out that morning. She told him she has to explain about the hospital. At the time of her pregnancy, she used an assumed name, Novelette Masters at both places, Sisters of Mercy and the hospital. She had traced her baby through the computer records. Based on those that gave birth on September 7 and 6th that possibly if the Dunstons have documents it must be forged. She never signed for Peter. They should produce those documents. She had gotten a form sent for a copy of Peter's birth certificate but in the name Ethan Gabriel Chimes, however, cannot remember if it came. Maybe Sister Grace or Katherine may have answers. When you cross examine the sisters, be gentle. Those women were my confidant and support when I hurt from loss of love and loss of children.

Martha is unsure of what will happen but has confidence that all will work out. Today made it clear what she has to do. The fear she had when she heard Maya was at Lenox Hill made her panic. At all cost Maya will have her kidney and as popular culture states do it afraid anyway. She is praying and believing in God. He will see her through. She remembers Peter walked on water and only started to sink when he took his eyes off Jesus and let doubt come in. She will remember Jehovah is God of the impossible and miracle working God. For good measure grabs her Bible and reads Matthew 14. Peter walking on the water, Luke 10:29 -37. The Good Samaritan. Isaiah, 41:10. And Philippians 4, verse 13. I can do all things through Christ that strengthens me. She feels fortified. She starts to sing Psalm 150 as taught by Nana who swears Noel Dexter was the original artist. She finds it on Google as she sings O praise yet The Lord, praise God in his sanctuary finds it invigorating, exciting and enjoyable.

Her bodyguards (BGs) have class social today- dancing their gym. The coach and other teachers will be there. It should end at 7:00, so the boys will get home a little late. She loves them dearly but today is a day of reflection and realization of what must be done. She is seriously considering withdrawing the injunction. She still feels the same way about possible effect on Peter but, it seems gross thinking about it; it being against your own mother is steep. If discord abounds, how can there be unity? She especially was always with her mother because Grandma Gertrude seemed to pick on her mother. She remembers one time asking, Grandma, why she didn't like mother. She denied it, saying it was just her way. Martha remembered how she used to tease her mother, how her eyes would light up when she heard Dad's key in the door. She would literally pat her hair and look down at her dress and throw the apron at her. He would always kiss the prettiest girl that was ever born. There were good times. All That ended after she started modeling and being Ogwin's girlfriend. What crap! Yet we women still do that. And for what? Many times, the men are as insincere as the clock that strikes 13. But every century a couple of good ones are born like Dad.

On cue, the phone rings. It is Adrian. "Hello, my lovely, how are you today?"

"Working to be terrific. Thankful God woke me up. How about you?" she said.

"What's that?" he asked.

"What's what?" she asked.

"I hear nothing. You mean my nemeses are not there. Alright, sounds terrific!"

Martha laughs. "Well, they are out until about 8:00 pm. It's already 5:00 pm."

"We can grab dinner and get to a movie. What do you want to see?"

"You assume I want to go," she teased. "Plus, you don't even know if I haven't already eaten."

"Well, pardon my excitement, I thought the Lord was showing me favor."

"You sound like a little boy whose father said yes, then changed his mind and said no."

"If you can find it in your heart to help that little boy you will cheer him up immediately," he begged.

"Are you begging Adrian?" she asked.

"Yes, he said. If you could see, you'd see me on my knees," he said earnestly.

"In that case I will go with you."

"Great. Pick you up in ten," he said.

"Ten! Where are you?" she asked.

"Never mind. Ten minutes!" he hung up.

Martha puts on a pair of Jeans. It is snug and is happy the B Gs are absent or else they'd suggest another attire. At the last minute, change to her gold blouse that has a peacock looking tail. It covers most of her derriere. That is strictly to appease her BG's. Exactly ten minutes her buzzer sounds, and she responds she's on her way down. She calls Keisha to tell her she's going to dinner and the movies. Keisha wanted to know if her tails are aware. She admonishes Keisha not to start.

"Hello gorgeous, I was trying to throw you off giving you ten minutes but you look great yet you couldn't have known I would call."

"Thank you. I just needed to don some clothes, brush my hair and get some lipstick and I'm done," she said."

"Really. Your face says otherwise."

"I'll confess my secret is Mary Kay Cosmetics. I quickly put on oil magnifier in the T zone, put on CC cream, quick flick of mineral powder, lipstick five minutes. Grab a pair of jeans, a blouse and sandals four minutes."

"It's amazing your face doesn't look like it needs a spatula to take the extra gooky stuff off."

"Well, my mom uses M Kay as do I and have no problem with it. It's great makeup. If you see these Mary Kay directors and consultants, their faces are unreal. I try to emulate them, but I don't have the patience. Mom takes fifteen minutes just for her face alone when she's getting dressed. She's a walking billboard for Mary Kay."

"So, if she wears it that well, isn't there a way to become a Mary Kay lady?" he asked.

"Get with the program. The word is beauty consultant. She says when she retires, but now she says she loves the pampering the consultant gives her facials and hands and leg treatment. Said the Foot Energizing Lotion does exactly that," Martha said."That's nice for me. Now I'm debating about continuing as a dietitian or going into the ministry."

"Oh, so what are you doing now?"

"I have a job at NYU Medical Center, but the debate rages on. There are lots of things you need to learn. There's a whole field of social justice classes you have to do and sadly, different religions while learning the scriptures. Honestly, I've done most of the religious, social justice classes and you must be a people person that's crucial and be open and reliable to so many issues. And most of all submit wholly and committed to the name of Jesus, His salvation and the love of God. You have to be all in, according to popular culture," she said

She finds Adrian looking at her and their eyes meet before he shifts back to the road.

" Yes, it's not just a career is it. Therefore, must not be entered into lightly, just like marriage, total commitment."

She nods. "That's about the size of it. Do you keep banker's hours?"

"I am a hardworking man. Many times, it goes beyond the 9:00 to 5:00. Do you see potbelly."

"No, but that doesn't mean anything. Maybe your metabolism is such it works it off easily," she said.

He laughs. "We are going to see Mission Impossible. The Reckoning, Part 1. We'll get Japanese and make it for the 8:00 pm movie at Village Cinema."

"Great. So, the BGs will know just where to find us."

"Are you serious? Oh. You're pulling my leg", said Adrian.

"Just wanted to see your reaction."

"In that case, no dessert. For that, no ice cream. No pastry. I might relent and get you some popcorn if you behave for the rest of the evening."

She shrugs her shoulders as he maneuvers himself in a tight spot. They are seated with menus all these huge portions as if you can feed four or six people with one of these dishes. "Is there something we can share? I don't want all that. It's gonna go straight down from my lips to the hips. I don't think so."

"What's wrong with your hips?"

"Forget I said anything. Move on, Boone and not a word," as he was about to say something.

He smiled, "sure," with even white teeth gleaming. He's too good looking for his own good.

"Your pleasure. I'll order lamb, ribs or maybe fish and we can sit close."

"Pardon me. You would sit by yourself. Fish indeed!" she said.

In the end, they're share ribs with brown rice and veggie medley. She orders fried chicken wings for the BGs.

"These are not for me," she said defensively. "I am thinking of your health and longevity."

"Thank you my sweet. What would I do without you?"

At 7:30 they are standing online when he suddenly turns towards her and kisses her. She is startled and grabs his arm for support. "What was that about?"

"Oh, I saw Walter. Not in the mood for a double date, I'd rather have the BGs," he said effecting a shiver.

The movie was good. Cruise didn't disappoint. She always had a thing for Vin Rhames when first she saw him in the movie Rosewood years ago with her dad. She loved the stunt he did with the horse. They waited until most patrons left before, they went out. The evening is balmy as they exit.

"Any sign of your buddy?" she asked, looking around.

"Thank heavens, no. He called me one day, said he saw you." He said watching her.

"Yes, he did. The day after, I was jogging and saw him on 6th Ave and 17th. I didn't stop to talk long, as I kept jogging on the spot to discourage talk. Made some comment about me being the sly one coming from nowhere to catch you so, tell me you got loose from somewhere. Why? Did I catch you?"

"Umm, what else did he say?"

"He asked where you were. Told him I didn't know but probably home. The light changed and I was able to go"

"You didn't say anything yeah," he said lightly.

"No, I didn't. Considering your actions today, with your look of tolerant indulgence, gathered you were not a fan." she said.

"You are right, I'm thinking others would mention it."

"Really, why your job depends on it. Or do you work for his daddy?"

"Are you being facetious?" he said.

"Impudent. Maybe. I don't think I'm likely to run into him too often. I like it when I'm not the center of attention. The only exceptions are and (gestures with her hand) and repeats the only exceptions are...."

"Me, myself and I," he said, laughing.

"For that, I will turn the BGs on you," she said. Let me call them."

"I'm sorry. Please don't. Please. It won't happen again."

"Okay, I won't," she said. And he entwines his fingers with hers and turns towards Union Square. There is always action there, impromptu concerts of talented street artists. Someone is always. imitating Michael Jackson, the moonwalk still fascinates every age group, or Jerusalem or the electric slide. Some people even break dance to it. They watch mimes as well as card tricks. Of course, you cannot count out the Jamaicans or reggae music. Someone's always singing One Love by Bob Marley or Bombastic by Shaggy. It was a delightful evening. And they walk slowly back to the car.

"We can walk home if you like, because finding a parking spot on your block is like finding a snowflake in summer."

Of course I would take my peace offering with me. But let me text them just so it doesn't appear you are a bad influence on me. Right. And when he doesn't respond, repeats, right!"

"Right," he said. What are you going to do when you get home?"

'Read and listen music till I fall asleep. You?"

"Read financial report if I feel like it. Tell me about you."

"Why?

"I barely know you, anything about you."

"Pot calling the kettle black."

"At least you know my address, my BG's and my friends. That we are all professional women that are employed and I am in divinity school. I'm in court on a secret issue. By the way, it occurred to me that you are wary, and I can feel and see you looking on me. Why?"

"Well, you interest me deeply, but I get the feeling you are careful about letting people in. Well, I live at E 22nd Street. I'm an investment broker, married once. Didn't fare too well. The only child of the marriage daughter Rose, died of pneumonia. She was 5. That's what kept us together and after she passed there was no reason to stay."

"I'm so sorry Adrian. That must be very hard. She hugs him. I bet she was a daddy's girl."

They stayed that way, then finally moved on. Thank you for sharing that. I'm sorry I didn't mean to pry."

"It's okay, it would have happened or come up sooner or later. Prefer it sooner. There are sometimes you seem afar off and then your face changes and there is the glimmer of a smile," he said encouragingly.

Martha instinctively knows he is inviting confidence. He wants her to reveal something. She is almost sure Walt told him what he implied when they met. She said, "one day, when the sun is up and the clouds are barely there, I will tell you. But there is enough painful memory for one night, and that's a promise."

And the night lost its gaiety and the mood is somber despite what he reveals about his personal life. She feels they reach another plateau in their relationship but cannot let anything derail her from her purpose. She wants to serve God and worship Him, follow His rules and love her neighbor as herself. It's for this reason she has to examine why she's seeing him. She knows deep inside she longs for a companion, but is he the person she is supposed to date. Lord, save me from me. Let me hear you, Father, I pray.

Adrian watches Martha. Her face is very expressive. He knows she is thinking about them, her future or her past. He is not shocked about what Walter revealed, but he has to admit that it's not the first thing you would say on a date. Is she afraid of being judged? Is that why she so dedicated to these young men and what of being in court? What is all that about? She goes to Lenox Hill Hospital often. Who is it she is visiting and why does it seem like she is in disguise? He cannot ask. She seems unaware she's being followed earlier. She seemed to think so because she looked around. He remembered the day she came out of the hospital; her head wrapped with scarf flowing from her head. She was wearing scrubs, but that scrub didn't hide that shape, whatever his Superiors believe she did, he was equally sure she didn't do it. She he hopes and prays that she reveals her painful memory soon.

"Martha, do you think the chicken wings will do the trick with the BGs. So, we can go to Prospect Park tomorrow?

"Umm. Well, Adrian, don't you have to work? What time will you leave?" she asked.

"Well, you could say tenish. I'll go to the office for two hours, then pick you up. Are you game? When she hesitates, be spontaneous, tomorrow will be a perfect day, not because I say so, but God made it."

"I need to prepare. Check my calendar, things like that before I can say yes. Besides, I would have to get lunch."

"You only eat salad."

"Even so, I prefer to make my own lettuce, tomatoes, cucumbers, pecans, croutons, carrots with a sprinkling of ham or chicken, sparkling lemonade and water. For snacks I need grapes and apples."

"He laughs. Well. You can get all that before we leave, if you insist," he said.

"Then I will get you what you want to eat. What's your pleasure?" she asked.

"Steak and potatoes, lobster on the side, asparagus or a veggie medley. he said, smiling. "I know you can handle that."

"Wait. Bend your head. She touches his forehead and neck. Umm, not running a temperature so since you are not feverish, you are wide awake but dreaming," she said.

Adrian laughs, "Why?"

"Really. You gotta be dreaming, fella," she said. "You spent a lot of time in the sun today."

"And here I think you want me to be happy."

"I do, but man, I have to take a look at you again in daylight."

They reached her apartment, he said he will circle the block, and goes down W 14th next, then go back, then up W 13th, and back on his 6th Ave and circle again to W 11th and to 12th. This time a car is pulling out.

"Victory, he shouted. I believe the block likes me. I seem to get parking more often than not. And after all that, I get stopped by the BGs," he said as he opens the door.

"Boys. Charles, Gabriel!" She moves to the bedroom. It is empty. Adrian, give me a minute. I am going by Sasha. She takes the chicken wings with her. She raps on the door. Sasha recognizes the special rap.

"Are my children in there?"

"Yes."

"Sleeping?" said Martha.

"Better be," Sasha said.

"On punishment, yes?

"They got in at 9:00 pm, thought their other mother was home, but fortunately on a date, so they are on punishment."

"Alright, I'm not interfering. I'm not the interfering type, you know that. Sasha snorts at that. This is for them. Can I at least kiss them?"

"You know Marty, you are the best and worst godmother/ Auntie. You spoil them."

"Well, I am accustomed to getting kissed nightly by two men. That's what puts me to sleep." "You need one, so you'll get one."

You separated them, Sasha! Why? That's double punishment." She leans forward, kisses Gabriel, and he smiles by murmuring her name. As Martha leaves the room, he says, I love you."

"I love you. But the spell you have on that boy must be seen to be believed. They embrace you."

"Are you asleep? she said. Did you help yourself to a drink? Can I get you something to drink or eat?"

"Yes, I'd like kiddies' champagne."

"Do you know, what a good chaser to that is, Sparkling lemonade. Wanna try?" As he nods, she gets two wine glasses from the kitchen, goes to her portable liquor cabinet, pours sparkling cider and lemonade. She had tricked the boys' years before and the name stuck. She's surprised Adrian remembered the name. She hands him his glass.

"Well, is it good or is it good?" she said proudly.

"Not bad, it's really nice. Come sit. The only thing missing is the fireplace as Sade croons in the background. They sit, not talking but at ease. She knows he is looking at her and closes her eyes. A smile plays around her lips as she realizes why she loves her BGs. Nothing will ever happen between her and Adrian, and she is glad.

"What are you thinking about? A person could write a story just watching the changes on your face. One-minute serious, next smile, somewhere far, then another smile and just a pleasant expression. Tell me what were your thoughts before I interrupt?"

"Sure, you want to know. You may need to pay cash for that because I don't accept checks or credit cards. My BGs are on punishment. Then their mothers separated them, and for once the other mother did not intervene. She just kissed her godson. He knew

I was there. He mumbled my name to the chagrin of his mother. She swears to disown me every day, but she is afraid she'd lose her son too. I've been hugging and kissing him since he was born." She smiles. "But he's a good kid. Are you ready to pay?" He shows her a 5 she shakes her head. Then he shows her a ten, twenty and still she declines. He offers a ten and a twenty together and she declines. He gives her a fifty (50) and she thanks him. "Nice doing business with you," she said.

"You are a cheat, a real con man," he said.

"Here's your mistake. You never asked the price for the information. You never negotiated the price Mr. Financier, so I earned $50.00 in minutes."

He tries to take it back and she pockets it, putting it in that snug fitting jeans where nothing moves.

"Come sit a little closer."

"I don't think so. You will try to pick my pocket. Okay, but don't try it, Boone. She rested her head on his arms. His face breaks in a smile.

"What are you thinking?" he asked softly.

"You will need more money."

"Umm, he said. Really. Let me see. Don't trust me?"

"Yes, but the money states in God we trust, and all others pay cash."

Adrian laughs and laughs. "Well, at least you make me laugh without antics. I like you a lot," he said, turning her to him and kissing her softly; "a lot," and pulled her closer. Martha doesn't fight him, even when he deepened the kiss. When he finally raised his head, she was limp. Things are stirring up in her, feelings she thought died in Bedford Hill. The type that gets you in trouble. She pulls away from him and he pulls her back and softly nibbles her ears and her head titles back of its own volition and he nuzzled her neck. Oh goodness what is happening to her? Her body's playing traitor to his lips, and her mind screams no, you know nothing about him. And the evil says what does it matter? He's arousing feelings deeper than you know you had. His hands moved suggestively and seductively.

"Oh no Adrian, please don't. This is crazy. We don't know each other as well as all that please. This is wrong."

"Why, we are consenting adults?"

"Yes, but we have to be responsible adults too. I can't go where this may lead to, you know, once you cross that particular threshold, you can't go back. I need to be true to my promise to serve God, be an honest Christian. I don't want to let emotions, genuine or otherwise befuddle my purpose. You don't even know me, Adrian. You don't even know who." She stops.

"So, tell me, let me decide. These feelings I have for you didn't start tonight. That day I saw you in Prospect Park, my whole world turned upside down."

"Oh, Adrian," she said. I can tell you that's lust. Lusting after the flesh there's nothing sacred about that."

"What are you talking about? It's not just lust. If it were, I'd have been all over you a long time ago. I wanted to get to know you and didn't want to scare you off. Tell me you felt nothing that you didn't enjoy that."

"So elder Boone you don't know sin is pleasurable? Why do you think so many people gravitate towards it? Why so many are caught up in it? Yes, I enjoy it. I had feelings I thought were dormant". She stopped and put her hand over her mouth when she realized what she revealed. She turns away and he comes up behind her, pulls her body back to him. He kisses her hand. And she closes her eyes. Suddenly she feels something hard's on her back and jumps.

"Don't worry," said Adrian dryly. It's only my belt buckle." And Martha falls out. She laughs so hard.

"So happy I can provide the amusement," he said smiling, and Martha continues laughing.

"Oh, I'm so sorry," she said. But neither her face nor actions verify the statement. Well, for what it's worth, it put a hold on to what could have resulted in dire consequences.

"I will leave just so I put my libido in check." He holds her hand and she walks to the door. She is still laughing silently so her chin is down. He raises it and bends to kiss her but the smile on her face makes him pause. "Guess, I have to learn new things with you, like how to kiss goodnight when someone's laughing." She stops and offers her lips, but the eyes are a giveaway. So, he kisses her forehead, and as her mouth opens in surprise, he kisses her. There was passion but controlled. As he lifts his head, their eyes lock, each searching and probing for what? This is a complication she is not willing to handle. With a chaste kiss, he lets himself out and she is standing alone, bereft of his lips and physical presence.

She tries to quieten her thoughts. She did not do anything wrong. She's got answers that she is human. And more so, a woman responding to a man. Well, temptation is all around as long as she doesn't yield to temptation, she feels safe. She knows what didn't happen that could have been was not due to her strength. She thanks God he put the restraint on Adrian. Adrian Boone the man with the seeking eyes. One thing, she reminds herself she's not going to succumb to lust, so she'll just have to keep far from him. If she were honest before he started kissing her, she was thinking the only thing missing was a fireplace and Nat King Cole singing, Chestnuts Roasting on An Open Fire and Christmas of course. Did she subconsciously wish to find out if he's attracted to her? She hopes not, but she's going to put the kisses to bed; instead put seasoning on the chicken breast she planned to cook earlier.

Martha changes to her favorite gospel singer, then changes and changes her mind a second time and finds Hezekiah Walker on Google. She needs the energy of that video in the square. As she watches the group she's swept up in Every Praise to Our God. She repeats it three times and then reads one of her consolation passages, Joshua 1 verse 9. According to Pastor, it's a great courage booster for when you are afraid, unsure and to dispel fear. She finishes with the Our Father prayer, because she really needs to be delivered from evil. Her sleep is punctuated with periods of waking for no reason. Her mind goes to Maya. The next time up, her mind goes to Adrian. She's almost certain he was in our dream. She cannot remember exactly where they were, what they were talking about why she was in court. He wanted to know what she was hiding. Walter told him about her. Well, she knows what to do once they meet.

Adrian remembers how Martha felt in his arms. She was responsive and he got a feeling of satisfaction. He's too old for unrequited love. His teenage years he was an active young buck and slowed down after marriage. And look what it got you, he thought sardonically. No, that's not fair. Rose was the love of his life. She was a daddy's girl. He smiles. He hopes his raging libido does not close the door with Martha, but he's leading a double life with her. If he were sensible, he wouldn't have got so personal. He should know better but, she is really beautiful and is so calm with it. What was she like ten years ago? No matter. He calls her and asks teasingly if she is still sleeping. She said no because of an early morning date with destiny and no worries she went jogging. He will get her at 10:30 am.

It is already 9:30. She is glad she used the mallet on the chicken breast. In another half hour, they will be finished. She has pita bread, garden salad with grapes, strawberries, apples and oranges. She has an insulated carry- all and puts the other food in and will add the chicken last. She can smell the jerk seasoning. Well, she is undecided about what to wear. She can wear her white pants but weary of grass stains. She decides on army green pants with a beige blouse. She adds a pair of beige sandals. As the time draws near, she gets aluminum foil for the chicken. At the last minute, adds another wheat bread. She has everything for their picnic including plates wipes and hand sanitizer. The journey to Prospect Park is uneventful. The talk is lively as they discuss sports; basketball, football, golf, tennis and the young Coco climbing in the rankings. Of course, his first love for tennis is Serena, hers is Venus. Those two are so phenomenal that if they play, she has never rooted against them. She remembered her father talking about Billie Jean King and Chris Everett. Those are his favorites and Arthur Ashe as well. Her dad bought his book A Hard Road to Glory. The next discussion is country music. He loves the old ones like Johnny Cash, Marty Robbins, Kenny Rogers and others. She likes Dolly Parton, Reba, Oakridge Boys, Kenny, Clint Black and others. Her father has a collection of Marty Robbins, and her favorite is El Paso. With gentle teasing, he sings with the radio.

They go to the Botanical Garden, searches and finding a big tree spreads out a quilt. They sit under the tree with Adrian stretched on his back with dark glasses.

I like that it's not sweltering yet, he said. What's for lunch? he asked. She smiles without answering. "Hey wench. What's for lunch? Can't you hear my stomach rumbling?"

"Oh, that's your stomach. I could have sworn that somebody just passed by on a bike, but in that case, here's chicken, cheese, grapes, and strawberry. There is salad and bread. What's your pleasure? She uses the sanitizer and picks up a plate. He will eat the strawberries and grapes but he is in need of pampering. She is to feed him. She moves closer and then he wants a pillow.

"You are out of luck. I do not have a pillow. Here I am thinking you are a rugged outdoor type and you get to Brooklyn and you want a pillow?"

"Have you ever heard of improvise? Let me show you. He puts his head in her lap. Just, making it easier for you to feed me. See how considerate I am?" "

"Of course you are," she said.

"And all see that no ants, bugs, flies, or any such insect bothers me. I will take a nap shortly," he said.

They chat while she feeds him grapes, then strawberries.

"That's a big strawberry. Share it with me; half and half."

She looks for the knife to cut it but, he said this way. He has half in his mouth and offered her the other half. She graciously takes it and smile.

"Full o' tricks, aren't you Boone?"

"And I think I am being original and will impress you. Frankly, I think it's genius, no."

"Of course, Boone, simply genius."

He points to his lips and picks up a napkin and pats them.

"You are a spoil sport. I have not worked so hard since the army to Impress a lady."

"No worries. I give you A for effort and B for results. Genius marks, I tell you", she said, laughing. "Why are you working at impressing me?"

"You don't know. I'm interested in you, woman."

"Really. I am interested in climate change," she said cheekily.

"You are sassy."

"Well, if you want a docile girl, it ain't me. I'm lively."

"Just for that cheek you need to keep the bugs off me, mosquitoes and flies so I can sleep. And as pay you get to watch me sleep."

She rolls her eyes without answering. Lying on his back and opening one eye, looks at her and smiles. Then he turns on his stomach, turns his face towards her, and wraps his arms around her waist. In about five minutes he's fast asleep. She puts in her earphones and listens to three songs and then listens and watches WhatsApp videos. She rests her back against the trunk and watches for critters as well as the brightly colored birds. She's plotting to drop some water in his back and pretends she does not see or know when if he opens his eyes.

"You are nice to sleep with. No snore, no tossing and turning. Great pillow. Thank you." Sitting halfway up kisses her. The actions bring back the night before. They eat a healthy lunch with lemonade. After they eat, she offers sugar free gum, mints and water. They sit back-to-back, bracing off each other. Then later they lean against the tree.

"Have you checked in with your BGs."

"No. They are in class."

"You mean they are not going to jump from behind a tree? I have you all to myself. What a treat" he said entwining their fingers."

"See how lucky you are?"

"Yes," he said, and pulls her on his lap. She anticipates his next move and as he bends towards her face, she holds him, by the chin and said, "say ah."

He opens his mouth, and she looks in and sniffs. Adrian laughs so hard she is thrown off his lap.

"I must be nuts. Where did your parents get you?"

She shrugs quite unrepentant, with a smile playing on her lips.

"Hey, Boone, changed your mine," she said, laughing while bending over him. He pulls her down, kissing her and rolling her on her back at the same time. She is trapped by his body. He leisurely kisses her. This time she is not going to think about flat abs, muscular legs or marauding tongue or caressing lips. At least she can try. She is telling her body don't enjoy the hard plains to her softness. Boone knows he's poaching on inhibit land. She relaxes too much and is a willing recipient to what he is giving. His hands roam her body, suggesting and delighting at the same time. She is drowning and is feeling powerless. She has never reacted to any man as she reacts to him. What's she thinking. There hasn't been.

"Oh Boone," she breathes. Stop. We can't do this. I'm so sorry. We can't." Even the birds stop chirping and the squirrel ceased their chatter as in empathy for their halted passion. It is like earth stopped and all collide and are in silent symphony.

"You are right, he said. It's neither the place, nor the time. Is there any ice I wonder."

"It won't help. The pond is around the bend," she said attempting humor.

"You gonna join me?"

"Go by yourself. I'll wait. I don't know what's come over me. Listen, Adrian, I've never reacted to any man as I do you," she said earnestly. I don't want you to think I'm loose or easy. I realize we have to stay three feet apart because bad things happen when we are closer."

"That depends on perspective. You are a young red-blooded woman if you think I am sorry for waking up the passion in you, oh no. You gave the impression of being aloof and cool but under that veneer pulse a desirable woman. And I am happy I found it."

He moves towards her, and she said, "Get away from me, Adrian," and moves out of his reach. "You seem bent on derailing my plans. Until I get a God wink just stay away from me. You are no good for my peace of mind and good sense."

"We will see," he said. Alright, I'm not making any promises. I think about you all the time, so I don't think you are any good for my equilibrium. I will be distant. (She brightens) for as long as it's possible, that is."

She shakes her head and looks across the distance.

"Two times you make reference to when you were away. Your friends did too, and the long look passed between you. Do you want to tell me now since it's daytime?"

She takes a deep breath and begins: Ten years ago, I was charged tried and convicted of a crime I didn't commit. I was at Bedford Hill Women's facility. Through many prayers and works by persons outside and the Warden I was paroled. I called my cousin Charlotte to get an appeal going. I didn't want to be paroled. I wanted to be cleared. There were discrepancies, foul up with evidence. DNA was not done on bloody garments or from under the Judges nails. No weapon was found on me or anywhere- witness disappeared. They forgot the cut I got defending Judge Frontes. (She shows her right hand) And everytime I tried to tell the lawyer, anything at all, it was wait, or said he knows. I told him about the person I saw in the hoodie. And the gentleman I passed, and he came when I called for help. And the clothes and whatever else was lost was, was found so Charlotte could use it. I went to see the quack masquerading as a lawyer and confronted him with the truth. I told him I know you were paid off that whatever woman you sell me out for hope she's worth it. But ten years free and he looked like crap. Old wrinkled and shriveled and ten years in jail I still get wolf whistles. That he will suffer even more. And the good thing I wouldn't have anything to do with it. I read the Psalm and I put the situation and him in God's hands. My God said I will give you beauty for ashes and then he said further, vengeance is mine, I will repay. So don't worry. God is amazing."

"You have my sympathy."

"Haven't thought much of him since then."

He walks up behind her and turns her around, lifts her chin and hugs her. "I am so very sorry."

"Thank you. So that's not something that crops up in conversation. The fact that I'm out of jail is nothing to brag about, or wear like a talisman. Ten years of my life was taken from me. I cannot get it back. Your friend might have seen me on GMA and The View.

"You haven't seen your lawyer you said since that day."

"No. I did a step and drew back, and the way he cowered in the corner, I told him don't worry. I would never touch him, there's not enough water in Manhattan plus the Hudson to get my hands clean if I did."

"Ouch.

"Yes, I went by myself but, I had tracking. The entire conversation is on file. He has his problems because he gets to live with himself. How's that for punishment? My prison was physical but his, is mental torment. Just hope he repents."

"Honey, that makes no difference to me. You said yourself God is awesome. You believed and he delivered you. You knew you didn't do it. Now the world knows it. But I'm sorry for your ordeal. We have an imperfect system but you survived and are thriving," he said.

"Yes, God is good all the time. All the time God is good someone came up with it that so, I hold that. That's why I can't afford to mess up and despite everything how I respond to you, I'm not going to yield to that temptation. Do you know, people think that's what Paul's thorn in his flesh was. Some said it was physical impairment. But whatever it was, Paul survived it though not on his own, but through the power of the Lord."

"Okay, preacher. Wanted to stay longer. We can stay till dusk. You eat like a bird anyway, so we have enough food."

"You don't know anything about me, she said, wagging her forefinger. No, I need to use a restroom, but this late it may be horrendous. We can find Grand Army Plaza Library or Brooklyn Museum.

"What makes you think they'll be any cleaner?"

"Probably not, but I prefer my chances there. They have a janitor on staff, okay," she said.

He seems to like holding hands. They get to the car and drive to the library. As they make their way towards the restroom a child about eight-ten asked if she was on tv. She asked if she was sure or maybe someone that looked like her. The child said if she had seen her standing, she would know. Martha asked

"Really. And why is that?" she asked.

"Because I would remember your 'boodie', Your 'boodie' is big."

"Scat," she said, and the little girl runs.

Adrian is amused and looks behind her and opens his mouth and she cuts him off; "And you better not say anything if you want two feet to walk and not end up in an ambulance."

"Okay!" He zips his lips.

Before long they are on their way. She checks her phone. There is a message from Maya sent some two hours ago. She calls her. She asked about her health and school. She recovered from her stomach issue. She wants Martha to visit. She pleads so hard that she asked Adrian if he could detour through Parks Slope, they are in the area anyway. Once he agrees she tells her maybe for ten minutes. She will be there in five minutes. As she goes through the gate, he rolls down the window and whistles. She ignores him. And to think he complains about the BGs but, he is just like them mildly irritating at times.

She rings the bell and is greeted by Grandmother Mary. The two talk and Martha enters the den. Maya is in the recliner. "Don't move. You look so comfortable there," and kisses her cheek. I am sorry I did not see your text until now. But is everything okay. You look peaky; had dialysis today. I forgot. Is there anything I can get you?"

"No, I just want you here with me. I feel better when you are with me," said Maya.

"Okay. Come here," and helps her from the recliner to the sofa and pulls her in her arms. I want you always to feel better darling. How I love you Maya," she said kissing her forehead. She cradles Maya's body. How can she leave her child when she needs her. She sent Adrian a text, may need more than ten minutes. However, within five minutes Maya falls asleep. She holds her for the original ten minutes. As she sleeps, it seems she is having issues breathing. She calls Mary and tells her about Maya's breathing. She settles down and seems more relaxed after a few minutes. Mary says it's okay for Maya to sleep on the sofa. She takes her leave telling Mary she cannot stay.

As they continue home, she is quiet. Adrian looks at her averted face and asks if everything is okay. And to her dismay tears are cruising her cheeks. He touches her hand, and she doesn't respond.

"Why are you crying and who is Maya." She shakes her head.

"I will be alright."

He holds her hand and they drive in companionable silence. At home she goes to the bathroom and wipes her face. As she returns to the living room, Adrian mirrors her actions with Maya. She leans on his shoulder, and he holds her in a circle. "Do you want to tell Uncle Adri? I am a good listener and an even better consoler."

She settles in his arms. It feels right and she feels safe and sheltered.

"Maya is the person I went to meet in Prospect Park the day I met you. I was directed to her and I found her. She pushed me away at first. Then she got sick and called me. She's very, very sick. She needs a kidney, and I decided to give her one. From an earlier experience I distrust surgery and was terrified. I agonized, then prayed about it now, I started testing. I know I am her match but, the doctor's must do what they must. See I believe the call to find her was from God. I had the place and the name to find her. I believe God called me to her. She is barely seventeen and on dialysis. She gets so exhausted and tired after her sessions. She wanted me there today because she feels better if I am there. But she fell asleep in five minutes, and I held her for ten and then left. She seems to be getting slimmer and slimmer daily. My heart breaks for her. How are you with more on plenty?"

"I do not know what you mean."

"When you think you have enough trials. Major problems then something else equally serious happens." He nods and she gets up and walks to the window.

"Here goes! At sixteen I got pregnant and gave the baby up for adoption. Only it wasn't one child but twins. I didn't know because I had no prenatal care until my sixth month. So, Dr. Gruniche, knowing I didn't have prenatal care kept it from me. He was aware I agreed to adoption so he made quiet plans for baby number two, my son. It was a rough delivery, I kept going in and out of consciousness, blood pressure dropping the whole works. I know when Sarai was born but during the haze and fog, I delivered my son. The doctor denied it at first then said he was still born. But I heard him cry like he was calling out to me. Long story short I found my son, left him where he was and became his babysitter for roughly two years, so I know where he is. By the time I could fight for him you know what happened. Just so you know if I knew I was carrying twins I would never ever have thought of adoption. Twins had always fascinated me, so I never would part from them even if my parents were to ostracize me. Anyway, my daughter I did not know where she was, and I agonized over it and then I got the directions in a dream to find a girl called Maya. So, I did and now I know why I was to find her. The first time I saw her in Lenox Hill Hospital with her head tied, she looked and is the splitting image of my mother. I could not breathe, and my chest constricted. I feel it. Maya is my daughter. I believe Psalm 37: 4 He will give you the desire of your heart. All the dreams, and the person in the exam room that spoke, telling me to go to Prospect Park, she was there. No, it's not a coincidence. I introduced my parents, Nana and siblings to my son Peter. He knows me as his ex-babysitter not his mother. My mother filed for visitation. I filed an injunction to stop it because I don't want to cause chaos and disrupt him, and my biggest fear he might reject me. I want him to get to know me me first. Anyway, that is what you call more upon plenty courtesy of Nana.'

"Girl how do you keep your sanity? A lesser person would've caved," he said hugging her from behind.

"Yes, maybe but, you see why I had to be home for Maya's sake. Prison could not hold me. God knows my baby needed me and I needed to find my daughter. That's why He is the on time, miracle working God. So, I am still a bit scared for surgery but I pray for things to work out for Maya and I will mend fences with mom later. I love them both so much. I dream one day we will meet as a family. Peter was stolen not adopted, but I don't want him to hate me. Adrian, that is why I study the uplifting and faith verses to keep me going. See I have to walk with God. That is why you represent my temptation, just out of reach. In addition, there is too much baggage, and you do not need that. You wanted to know about me, here is me."

He tips her chin and kisses he softly. "No. What if God wants me there too so we can both bridge these challenges. Together we are stronger. We can do this."

"Will you go with me to Lenox Hill so I can give my daughter a second life?"

"Not even Mt. Etna, not wild horses can keep me anyway. Well?"

"I like that." And he pulls her closer. His heartbeat is steady and assured. And she feels it and gradually hers picks up his rhythm and together they beat as one. It's an old rhythm and timeless belief finding your ultimate love the hearts beat together.

Chapter 9

*a*s Adrian opens door he is able to face what he has been afraid to acknowledge before. He is not impotent as Isabella Frontes said. It has been a long time since he felt any physical attraction towards a woman. And in a matter of days, he felt this attraction to Martha; worse it is getting worse every day. So, Isabella, he snorted you are wrong very wrong. It was her deception that killed any fondness he had for her. Furthermore, she had lied about her pregnancy. As an investment broker among other things, the math didn't add up. After Rose's birth he permanently moved out of their bedroom. He told her he had a problem with Rose's birth as humans traditionally gave birth after nine months and had never heard of a baby six weeks overdue and an OB/GYN did nothing, and the baby not in distress and a myriad other complications yet, she is full term and birth was on time. Many women sought his bed and attention because of who he is not. He was turned off then and still is from New York elite and upper crust. They bored him. Their pseudo affection for each other, always competing always to be atop the social ladder; therefore, spending daddy's money and husband's money faster than it's minted.

But out of the blue, came Martha. A woman with a knockout figure, unaware of her beauty and charm makes him feel like twenty-one again. He has no right to think or feel that way about someone he is investigating. That is a big no-no. It seemed a good idea at the time to court her interest, but it backfired. He loved her. There he said it. He loved her so much, but he can't make his superiors know that. He will do his final report and recommend closing the file. She was not guilty, she didn't kill Dungkirk. Watching her for weeks and talking with her about what she had to hide was familial things. In addition, her bodyguards follow her everywhere. Look how hard he had to work to ditch them. She would not risk their lives. She is too protective of them. Even so, why did he have to fall in love with her. Dungkirk succumbed to his injuries much like Judge Earl Frontes; and coupled with her visit to see him gave rise to suspicion of coincidence or murder. She is no serial killer and that is what he has to prove and fast. His bosses forget DNA proved otherwise. Problem is he can't ask her what route she took to Dungkirk because she would want to know why. He has to find a street camera. Most likely she took the subway. Where did she go, to the F train or to Union Square. There she will have access to the N, R, 2, 3.4 and 5 going to downtown Brooklyn which involves Court St Metro Tech and Borough Hall.

One of life's irony he has to prove she didn't kill Dungkirk because his heart is involved. For the first time in a long time, he finds someone he can love, does love and he is investigating her. One thing is sure he is not giving her up. He is able to access the cameras, and he searches for hours the F train station 14th Street station. He finds nothing after three hours of intense search. He calls Jamal and asks him to search the entrances at the southern end of Union Square for Martha. With Jamal's help he can accomplish this in half the time. He begins to search opposite to Jamal's. They eventually quit but Adrian is sure they overlooked something. What if she went into the supermarket and took that entrance. That is the only footage they did not look at, and cameras were down. He will start again tomorrow.

He calls Martha asking about Maya. She tells him she is a match for Maya, but they have more tests to run; asking if she has any communicative diseases. She is tested for AIDS, TB, Hepatitis A, B, C and more she doesn't know the names of. He tells her through pressure of work he will be busy for the next two days however, if an emergency arises to call him. She promises and hangs up. Adrian decides to go in person to Borough Hall for direct access of the cameras, rather than remotely. He gives the Tech guy a picture of Martha. He is warned it is confidential. With the advanced technological software, it is easy to spot her. He needs fresh eyes. He does not want his desire to exonerate her, make him miss something. Jamal is also working on the cameras there. He has to get out because he feels agitation knocking.

On impulse he walks to the hotdog vendor and asks him if he has seen her. He assumes she is missing, and Adrian does not correct him. He believes he saw her a week ago at the Pierrepont Street exit. He thanks him and leaves wondering if he really saw her. Maybe Jamal and the transit tech worker may have something concrete by now. He knows she is not guilty but, doing this for the others to prove she's not guilty. They are poised to believe the worst. They are ignoring the DNA evidence that cleared her. Evidence was mishandled but, they are hardnosed, and have seen too much crime and corruption. Thence it becomes imperative to clear her, but how? They have uncovered nothing that is positive, except he has it on tape she visited her lawyer. He realizes he is panicking. He has to put some distance between them so he can look clinically at this. There must be something he is overlooking.

Though exhausted he calls and invites himself over. He needs to see her and touch her even for five minutes. He has been going for three days straight without a break. As he reached her door, it opens. Martha is standing there radiant.

"Hi stranger. Long time no sees."

"Lovely to see you. You look terrific."

"This ole' thing! Don't worry if the boys see you," she said turning away.

"Uhuh. Not so quick. I have not seen you in three long days," and kissed her. I am bone tired. I have deadline but, depriving myself of your company isn't working for me," he said as he pulls her to the sofa

"So, what am I, your work relief," said Martha.

"Mm, he said settling his head on her shoulder. I like how you smell- very nice."

He starts to shuffle and she asks what is wrong. He tells her he's settling himself to get comfy.

"Alright Adrian, lie on the futon, you'll be more comfortable."

"No. I like the pillow I have," he said.

"I will move the pillow for you. Be a nice boy and move."

She sits on the futon with him and he lies in her lap and his arms around her waist.

"Mmm, this is good. Thank you; better than the couch."

The even movement of his chest, and sigh tells her he is asleep. Well, he said he would visit for an hour so she will wake him within the hour. He must be doing some heavy investments for him to be this tired. She tries waking him at 6.45 pm and he mumbles he wants to sleep. At seven thirty she wakes him and he stretches and tells her, 'I like my bed.'

"Thank you for being so understanding and accommodating," he said kissing her. His lips lingers longer than he intends. He should quit while ahead before he embarrasses them both.

"When is your next court date," he asked.

"July 7th. Why?"

"I will drive you there," he said.

"That's not necessary. I'll hop a train and make my way like I did before. You know me, I am a Brooklyn girl. Love trains, I don't know why I didn't become a train operator," she said laughing.

This is the opening he was hoping for.

"When you go to Brooklyn which train do you take?"

Depends on where I am going; to see the parents it's the F to W 4th to B train; if Macy's can be the 4/ 5 or 2/3 depend on my feeling.

"How so?"

"Well number 4/5 from Union Square because it's express to Brooklyn Bridge then once you get to bowling green, next stop Borough Hall. Why are we talking about trains?"

"Nothing except you turn my offer down to take you to Westchester."

"You have to work or is that an assumption. You need to study the stock market so you can give good advice, right?"

"Yes. But I can from anywhere. I have my laptop and phone. I can watch stock movement and market fluctuation from anywhere, is all. So, do I pick you up?"

"Okay Boone. Court is 10:00am sharp. I'd like to be there at a quarter to, no later. And thank you for offering and I accept," she said laughing.

He takes out his phone and types.

"What are you doing?"

"This is to remind me I have an appointment next Wednesday July 7. Gotta go sweetie," he said kissing her cheek and he was gone.

That man is an enigma. She still thinks he is fishing for something. Guess he cannot understand she is very independent. She turns the radio to CBS FM 101.9. She likes the music they play: little jazz, rhythm and blues, Doowop and she has a new appreciation of songs from the 50's. Those groups could really, really sing. She remembered her dad saying how romantic those ballads were, and how he used to sing to her mom. I thought she married you for your looks she used to tease. That too, he'd say and they would both laugh. She missed that. That is why it is so important to build lasting memories for times like these. Look how she and her mother are distant now. It is ironic that her mother thought she preferred her dad, but it is because they have so much in common. They both love her and that is what they talked about. Her mom knew they talked about her without realizing the great love she had for her. Oh mom! And her ears caught the sounds of Betty Everette: Does He Love Me I Wanna Know and she listens to the Everly Brothers and sleep claims her.

Her visit to Maya twice per week became routine. They would visit Prospect Park. She was happy to spend time with her without the hovering/ interference of DC Sturgeone. She understands his concern though she made it clear to Maya if she went to Westchester, her father could accuse her of trespassing. He is protective of Maya, and he should but she believes he is suffering from midlife crisis? The male eagle can be so fragile at times. The wife's not paying enough attention to them, don't exhibit gladness when home. Rather than fight for their home/marriage they move out. She sighs. All this is speculation but concluded from bits and pieces from Maya. She wonders. She wishes they'd get back together for their children's sake as long as there is no physical/emotional abuse. She realizes she has never prayed for peace and the unification of Maya's family. So, in prayer, she asks for restoration and healing for families across the state, country and the world. Then she prays for the Sturgeone, the Dunstans, for her family, between her and mother, grandmother, and for herself with both her children, Maya and Peter. She asks for bridging the divide, for softening of hearts balancing on forgiveness.

Wednesday, July 7th seems to be in a hurry. Martha prays her Serenity prayer, reads Psalm 23, 121, 27, and Isaiah 41:10 to dispel the disquiet that's been plaguing her from the day before. She realizes what upsets Maya invariably upsets her too, despite the brave words she said to Maya. Her greatest wish is if she could love her wholeheartedly without guilt. Maya seems independent but clings to her. It is as if she is afraid Martha will leave. She does not understand the almost obsessive need for constant reassurance. Last night she told Maya that she is her first choice as a daughter. I love you that much, pumpkin. And for the first time, she believes Maya heard her and in her spirit was a shift. She has this serene look on her face as she bids her goodnight. Martha believed she heard. Goodnight, mom so soft she wondered if she imagined it. She turned the video off. Maya was asleep. So why is she feeling this way? She should be happy that Maya seemed settled last night and aware she is in court and will visit after. Adrian arrived at 8:45 am and they are off. They have plenty of time to get there. The sisters, Katherine and Grace, will be there to testify, Nurse Gretchen Whitmore, Nurse Radcliffe, Social worker, Andreesuis and the Dunstans. Since she testified before, is not scheduled to do so again. Adrian asks her if she is nervous or afraid of seeing her mother. She told him no. As they near the courthouse, he brings her hand to his lips telling her that she is safe. She is smiling as she looks at him. They have minutes to spare.

"Are you going to wait here until everything is over," asked Martha.

"It is no problem. There's nowhere else I'd rather be."

"But you can't even come inside Boone," she protested. Wouldn't your time be better utilized. I can't call or text you to say what is happening or how long."

"You worry for nothing. I choose to stay and just in case you need comfort or a getaway car, I'll be ready. It is no problem, Miss Chimes," he said softly.

She rolls her head to the side to look at him and is about to speak and he kisses her. After the kiss her hand on his cheek asks softly.

"What am I going to do with you?"

For an answer, he kisses her again. "I would tell you but you won't let me," he said. "Anything you want or desire is yours."

"Umm. Bye Adrian. See you later," and slips out before he could kiss her again. He calls her, but she doesn't look back.

"No Boone," she said.

"No to what?" he said, laughing.

As she enters the waiting room sees Nurses, Gretchen and Radcliffe. She hugs nurse Radcliffe and greets sister Grace and Sister Katherine. She enters the chamber and greets her parents, and the Dunstons, Esther obviously still mad at her. Judge Douglas enters and gives his opening remarks. Mr. Perry addresses the court saying that the injunction is withdrawn. He said it is a voluntary withdrawal with prejudice by Martha Chimes. The judge asked if there was any coercion. Attorney Perry denies coercion. The medical record from Bristol Street Clinic in Brooklyn is available. Martha asks for it to be held in case it is needed. The sisters from the home testified their ignorance Martha was having twins, as Doctor Gruniche never told them. They learned of it at EDC and believed Martha, although unbelievable that the Doctor who worked with them for more than 15 years deceived them. They were unable to contact the doctor shortly after. Nurse Radcliffe said she believed Martha that she had twins. When she heard about the stillborn baby knew that it was true as that happened the day before and stillborn was Esther Dunstan's baby. She told Martha stillborn baby was the day before September 6th. She believed it was cruel to show the dead baby to her/Martha. She was distraught. Social Worker Andreescies said she filled out the birth of record form as given her Ethan Gabriel Masters and wasn't aware of the controversy until later notes indicated two babies, boy and girl. She knew of the form signed for baby girl and adoption. There was no paperwork for adoption given to her for Ethan Gabriel. Nurse Gretchen Whitmore admitted everything from the plot to put the second baby up for adoption without the mother knowing, because he hid, she was having twins. She took the baby from the hospital in her gym bag. Doctor Gruniche was secretive about the adoptive parent but knows it was a biracial couple. And they were business people that the wife had multiple miscarriages. He referred to them as JD's. The Judge leaves for ten minutes recess.

For the first time, Martha feels her phone vibrating. She looks and sees it's Maya's number. There's a message. Maya, hospitalized, has almost complete renal failure. She makes a sound and tells Perry, "I have to go. It's a matter of life or death. Have to save my daughter, Apologize to the judge for me." She runs through the waiting room dialing Adrian.

"Please pick me up." She prays it seems like an eternity. He picks her up.

"Adrian, I need to get to Lenox Hill Hospital pronto. It's Maya. She's in acute renal failure.

Her next call is to Sasha. "Hey, Sasha. Have to be at Lenox Hill.Maya is very sick. Meet me there.

She sends text to dad. Had to leave due to medical emergency. Have to help a friend- later.

Adrian is at the courthouse steps, and she gets in. "Take it easy, honey, he said. I will get you there pronto."

She's so afraid. She can only nod. In twenty minutes, he's at Lenox Hill, she's about to walk away and he said, "No. We go together."

He holds her hand, and they go to the ER. They locate Mary and the Doctor, her neurologist. However, the nephrologist is with her.

"Thank you my dear, for coming. She missed her last dialysis session, but here's the doctor now," said Mary.

"I don't know. I'm sorry. He nodded to Adrian. I think I met you."

"Yes, said Mary. Martha is donating a kidney to Maya."

"Good, good. Yes, yes of course. We need to move right away. Miss Martha, I'm Doctor Calvin, George Maya's nephrologist. If you are ready to go, I can start in the hour."

Martha inhales and nods. She looks at Adrian and his fingers tighten over hers, then he hugs her.

"You will be okay. God is overseeing this one baby."

"Can I see Maya? I want her to know I am here." She kisses Maya. I am here. I am keeping my promise." Maya opens her eyes and smiles. "God is good to me."

Martha said to her. "This is Adrian. He's, my friend."

"Hello, Maya. You ready to get well? We will both be here. God grant you peace and blessings. His arms will keep you and your faith, you're healing."

As she beckons to Martha she bends as she whispers. "I like him, he's cute and handsome with pretty teeth. You can keep him."

"Thank you." Martha laughs, hugs and kisses her. "Rest now. The doctor is going to schedule the surgery for later this evening. Need another two hours to get rid of the tea I had this morning or so. I am here. Please rest, no more talking."

"What about court?" Maya asked

"I told my lawyer it was medical emergency, life or death, and I ran. Adrian brought me here. Rest Maya rest." said Martha.

Martha walks away from Maya a half smile on her lips. She sees him looking at her eyes narrowed.

"What did Maya whisper; and don't tell me nothing. You're avoiding looking at me says it's about me."

One look at his face tells her he will remember. She said you are cute, likes you and I should keep you.

He beamed. "Wow! she said that, which means you can't get rid of me. Yes!" he said hands clasped.

Martha's phone rings. It is Sasha. "Yes, Sash."

"I am here," said Sasha.

"Find the ER. You will see me. I will come to the open area."

They embrace and she waves to Adrian; Martha brings her up to date. They will do the surgery today. The team is there. It's to get an operating room cleaned and checked. In a while, a nurse comes to get both patients, and they are taken to the eastern section of the hospital. They are checked in and given wrist bands. Martha stops them asking if she shouldn't shower before the surgery. It's an emergency, yes but she has lotion on. She is not willing to risk Maya's fragile health or her own. Consequently, the nurse gives her wipes. Martha instructs Sasha to reach her back and she will take care of the rest.

"So, what about me? What do I do? Watch."

"I see you don't like yourself," said Martha. "Keep it up. You may get a bed here."

Adrian smiles and Sasha laughs.

"Don't laugh Sasha. Don't encourage him. Have you ever seen a six-foot nut? Now you have," she said pointing to Adrian.

She puts on two robes and Martha is ready. She removes her ring, chain and earrings, giving them to Sasha. She needs her phone, dress and shoes in a locker. The other things should go home. Soon they are ready, and they wield them to the big elevator. Adrian, Mary and Sasha go with them to the other waiting area where all information is double-checked: name, date of birth, reason and what type of surgery. The surgical team tell them they'll be put to sleep, given a preference of injection in the spine or through IV. Both elect IV. Martha asks that they go in together, holding hands. Before the last stage the parents come in. She waves to Adrian and Sasha, Mary and the parents. Two men enter, calling their names, and as they enter the area, Martha holds her hand smiling at her. The IVs are working. She is feeling sleepy. She hates the oxygen. It burns her nose. When Martha sees the lights, they appear to be swinging, making her feel dizzy. She hears the voice telling her to pull herself up, and she will, if she sinks into oblivion.

Martha awakes. Where the dickens are? What sort of place is this. As the fog clears, she sees shadows. She looks again and the place is bright.

"Adrian."

"Hi darling. I thought you'd never wake. I kept checking your pulse despite paraphernalia behind you."

"Where is Maya?"

"Maya is fine. She woke then went back to sleep."

"Please ring for the nurse for me." And Adrian lowers her back on the pillow. She's in 2W step down from ICU. The nurse arrives.

"Oh Ms. Chimes I am glad you are up. How do you feel? Thirsty and hungry or both. I'm nurse Patrick."

"Nurse Patrick please get a wheelchair, take me to Maya or I'll go unassisted to look for her myself."

As Martha beckons Adrian to help her to a sitting position, the nurse said she would let them visit. Martha requests for the doctor to visit as also. Nurse Patrick kept her word, and Maya is brought to the bed next to her. She thanks the nurse.

"Adrian, it's a long day. You should've gone home."

"Really. You think I'd leave without my talking to you- see that you are awake. No, my love."

Maya starts to moan in her sleep. Martha turns her attention to Maya.

"Maya baby I am here. I told you I am not leaving you. Please push the bed closer together Adrian so I can touch her. Thank you."

As Martha touches her, she becomes still. "I am here baby. I am not going anywhere," she said rubbing her cheek. Maya smiles and sighs in her sleep. And Martha knows she will sleep till morning.

"Anything I get you?"

"I don't think so. Maybe some peppermint tea. Maybe the nurse can tell you."

The nurse has peppermint and points him to the microwave. He boils the water and brings it back. Then he forgets the sugar but she tells him she does not take sugar with her tea. The tea is scalding and will burn her tongue. She will wait a few minutes. She is able to sip cautiously after three minutes. She asks him to tell the nurse to assist her to the rest room in addition she will need to void in a cannister that fits the seat to monitor output. She accepts the walker and Adrian accompanies her to the bathroom holding the door and pulling the IV pole for her.

"Oh gosh. I feel nauseous," she said. He hurries to her leading her to the basin and not too soon. She vomited the tea and everything else. He holds her. The nurse comes in, unhooks the IV.

"I came in, to pee but I felt nauseous and all the wonderful peppermint down the drain. And now my mouth taste blah. Do you think you can find a toothbrush and toothpaste." She rinses her mouth.

"Not to worry, I can help with that. Your friend Sasha tells me you are fastidious with your teeth. We bought a toothbrush and paste and mouth wash. Don't worry my sweet. It's all covered."

"Thank you, Dr., A or is it Nurse A? I appreciate it. They said the medication should last for seventy-two hours. Seems it is true. I am not in any pain, just nauseous. I take it Sasha left. Did you draw straws?"

"Yes, and I won. I'm a better Nurse P and I don't have to pacify the BGs," he said smiling. I could hold you if you want to sleep."

"Not yet. I have to call the BGs. They will not sleep otherwise my parents and Nana."

She calls Sasha and then the boys. She's groggy but not in pain, just nauseous. Adrian is monitoring her. She blows them a kiss and hangs up. She calls her parents. Her dad picks up. After pleasantries, tells her the Judge was angry and there's an 11:00 am call tomorrow and she must be there. She explained she is hospitalized and will text her lawyer in the morning. She can do a video call, but not much else, she explained. She donated a kidney to a deserving child. It was a life and death situation. That's why she had to run. I hope mom is hearing this but I am groggy and we'll talk tomorrow. She sends her love to all.

"You have exceeded your quota of calls, and it is nap time. Your eyes are glazed. I can hold you until you fall asleep."

He levers himself on the bed. And she puts her head on his shoulder. "Hold one minute" he says and kisses her forehead. She nestles and could feel his chin on her head. His arms encircle her and she is thinking how comfortable she feels and what a great pillow. Adrian watches her sleep as she moves her head to his chest. How peaceful she looks. She is carrying so much. God, grant you grace, health and peaceful sleep. During the hours he waited for surgery and recovery, he found the illusive footage. She emerged from the subway from the municipal building at 11:15. BND office supplies picked her up 11:20 according to Jamal. At 11:40, BND picks her up again. The Borough Directors office camera picks her up 12 noon. She enters Jay

St. Metrotech Subway 12:15. At 12:30 she is at 14th St. and 6th Ave. Martha is definitely in the clear. He will make his recommendation to his superiors while handing in his resignation.

Martha awakes and Adrian is holding her still. He must have dozed off and the steady rhythm of his heartbeat put her back to sleep. The next time she wakes he is flexing his arms.

"Oh Adrian, you stayed all night. You must be tired with aches and pain. And thank you for deciding to drive me to court. It was a terrific idea."

"Maybe. It was worth it. You look so peaceful and felt so good in my arms I did not want to leave you. Do you know I used to be normal until I met you?"

As she starts to laugh, she feels the plaster at her side. Blood is seeping through. She is unable to determine if it's fresh. The light is dim, so she could be mistaken. She calls the nurse and asks if she can look at her cut and if she can get some wipes. She asks Adrian to step outside and closes the screen. She turns on the light. The blood is dried. She asked for assurance. She is uncomfortable without underwear.

"Adrian, you should go home and get some sleep. You are a great nurse and companion. Then you can have late dinner with me tonight, she said.

"Okay," he kisses her cheek. "Your toiletries are in that bag. Remember we have a date. Don't go anywhere."

He bids the nurse goodbye and leaves. She gets warm wipes and a basin and the dish with mouth care. She uses the warm wipes and then goes to the bathroom with her toothpaste, brush and mouthwash. When she is finished, she goes by Maya's bed. She kisses her brows. She is sleeping peacefully still. Martha goes back to bed. She must look like fright night. She goes back and reads the Psalm and prays. She sends a text to her lawyer Perry explaining her present situation and offers video call. Well, she will be in gown with uncombed hair, but her teeth and mouth are clean, not that they'll care. Maya wakes and Martha helps to wipe her down. The golden hue from the antiseptic is still present. Fortunately, Doctor Calvin is early on his rounds by 8:00 am. He must make sure the kidney is adapting and functioning. Martha is confident God is on the job, making all crooked paths straight. She knows God will grant her favor.

She has the video call and makes her apologies to Judge Douglas and the others. She makes sure her IV, wristbands, bed and name tag are all showing. She will submit discharge papers, if necessary, the judge makes no favor of visitation since the injunction is withdrawn. The adoption is questionable at best; the fact that the Dunston's baby was stillborn the day before the baby they adopted was born. Given the adoption process can take years, the information will be given to the DA and a thorough investigation will be carried out. There are heavy implications against Gretchen Whitmore and the Dunstans and Dr. Gruniche. Transcript of yesterday and today's transcript may possibly go to the FBI. Peter must be told by the Dunston and visitation is July 25th. The bio-mother should aid the transition between grandchildren and grandparents.

Martha is glad the court case is over, but, laborious task ahead to unite a 17-year-old with his biological mother, grandparents and great Grandparents and aunts and cousins. She is not looking forward to the task. Lord, you have to take the lead on this because I have no clue. She repeats. Isaiah 41 V 10. She reads Jeremiah 1 and meditates on it. In the meantime, she watches over Maya. She tells her, to ask Mary to bring her toiletries and a comb. Adrian, Sasha and the boy's visit. The boys are introduced to Maya. Gabriel is friendly, asking Maya if now she has Auntie Martha's kidney, if that makes her a relative. Of course, his sidekick echoes him. The boys are openly demonstrative to Martha as usual and Maya watches them. On the third day Marthais about to be discharged. Her kidney is fine; working as it should. She cannot wait to take the Foley out. It is a nuisance. Maya gets upset and is crying. Martha tries to tease her out of her sadness, promising her she will visit, but not the following day. Because she needs positive outcome on her investment.

"Maya. Why are you crying like that? I will see you. You have to stay longer. Is there something someone said? You can tell me. I'll tell you differently. I don't understand." She sits on Maya's bed pulling her in her arms.

Sniffling, Maya says, "I know who you are. I saw you on TV last year and that's when I knew."

"Okay, you know who I am. I should hope so. We have been very close for a couple of months."

"That's not what I mean. I know you are my mother. The first time I saw you on TV, you looked familiar. And then I know why. You look like me. So, I heard you were going to be on The View and I got tickets. Then I asked The View to set up a meet and I was to meet you at that restaurant. I went but got cold feet. I watched you and you seemed sophisticated and I got scared, so I ducked out of the meeting. When I saw you at Prospect Park, I was afraid you'd know I stood you up. Plus, I had a disagreement with my parents. I didn't like that they were not loving anymore, and they always sarcastic to each other. Then my sickness getting worse, I didn't want to believe you that there was divine intervention even though I prayed to find my bio mother."

"Well, pumpkin, your prayer was heard and answered. My prayer was answered too. I always wanted to know where you were. I prayed Psalm 37: 4. He will give you the desire of your heart. I knew certainly you were my daughter the first time I saw you in the hospital with your head tied. You are a copy of my mother. I almost flipped. I could only thank God, I found you. So, the love I have all these years for a baby girl translated into a beautiful adult. I said I'll just continue loving you. What if you rejected me but once I had the connection, I vowed I'd never lose it. My beautiful Maya, my daughter, I told Sasha and Adrian, but none of my relatives know I was afraid of rejection. It's 17 years and not a day has gone by I didn't regret signing the adoption papers. But when you are well enough, we will talk more. I love you so very much."

"And I love you too, Mom."

"So, you did call me Mom the other day. I thought I imagined it," she said, tears streaming down. "I will never let you go, even if you are legally Sturgeone. Thank you for loving me so freely and undeservedly. Can I tell my parents and my grandparents I found you. I do not want you to be uncomfortable."

"Oh mom, once I am better, I would like to meet the whole family."

"Please remember if you don't, it's alright. If you have any reservation at all, say so and no hard feelings, my baby." She hugs her kissing her several times. She is ecstatic. She wants to tell the world.

"I still don't want you to go. I like you holding me and kissing me as if I'm precious."

"Of course you are precious, darling," Martha said.

"Are you going to marry Adrian? That's his name?"

"That's his name. But the marrying, I don't know why."

"I like him. I can tell he likes you a lot, the way he looks at you. It is not casual," she laughs.

"Really. So, is it like the M&M's commercial? With this song Hungry Eyes, do you remember it? Because I want to know if I should start running just like the M&M."

Maya laughs. "No, mom. It is a gooey look like you are so beautiful and I love you; that sort of look."

"Okay. I see you have a lively imagination. I am very fond of Adrian. He is the only person I've let get close to me in 18 years. I didn't want to be hurt again. I was 16 years old when I made a promise and kept it till, I met him. And it's unreasonable but refer to me as Mom in private. I don't want to hurt the Sturgeons, but please, for me. Promise? if you promise, I'll tell you a secret."

"Okay, I promise.

"Alright, let me get my phone. See this boy What do you think of him?"

"He's kinda cute. Who is he?"

It's your brother, your bio brother."

"What? Well, if you had only one pregnancy. But how come? Oh geez, twin! I am a twin. She said as Marta shushed her. That is awesome; how cool. No mom spill- give me the dirt."

Martha laughs. She tells Maya off the switch in babies and how she was able to track him down. However, she left him there because she didn't have any place to live. She was estranged from her family then, and she thought it was punishment for her adoption. Martha stayed an extra day in the hospital and bribing Maya, if she did not cry, would bring a gift for her the day after. She would FaceTime her four times the next day. Adrian picked her up mid-morning and took her home. It was a chore to bathe but did in installments and she slept for the remainder of the day. She dismissed him but he refused to go, so she left him to the two BG's. Due to special circumstances. Doctor Calvin wanted to keep Maya an additional two days. Maya was very upset.

Martha invites her parents to her home on Saturday and also Nana. She has to start preparing the family. They are introduced to the BGs, the WASP. There's couscous, cold cuts, jerk wings, cheese, crackers homemade turkey meatballs and Nana pineapple upside down cake, non-alcoholic beer, sparkling cider and lemonade. And a delightful addition Adrian Boone. She addressed them; she wants her parents and Nana to meet the people who are important to her, and considers family. The family will get bigger and better. And it is time to bury the hatchet to be a family again. Later the siblings, Jonathan Denise and Yvonne show up, which starts another round of introductions. Between the foyer, living room and kitchen all are accommodated. Adrian asked her to sit down or else he'd lock her in her room. She does, reluctantly sticking her tongue at his back. Nana is a witness and laughs delightfully. She likes Adrian. She must invite him over. They dispersed about 9:00 PM. She was tired but was the gracious hostess. Later, she tells her mother she has a surprise for her the following day, Adrian would pick her up at 1:30. pm. And dad to get there 3:00 pm. She is not to question Adrian for a clue. Adrian is to take her to Lenox Hill. Sasha and the BGs would be there to warn if the Sturgeone's turn up.

On Sunday, Maya calls Martha. "Are you on your way yet?"

"No Maya, I will be there at 2:30-ish. Watch the church service until I get there."

"That is forever," Maya wailed.

"I wonder where you get that dramatic flair. You exaggerate. Plus, Mary and your grandfather will be visiting and the time will go by fast. Or you can aggravate the nurses. Be patient."

"Mom, I am shocked, but it sounds like a good idea. Alright, I will try to be patient alright. The fighting Sturgeone's are here. Bye mom."

Martha is relieved. It is barely 10:3 0. The Sturgeone's are early. Maybe by 2:30 they will leave. She doesn't mind if Mary is there, but she feels the others tolerate her. She's happy. What she does is for

Maya, not anyone else. However, events were unfolding she knew nothing about. Her mother asked about the lady that donated the kidney, how she was doing and to give their regards and her father snorted that Martha is an impostor worming her way into Maya's life. So that started an argument with the parents. Sharon said she was grateful someone could save her daughter, and she had no right to judge Martha. I didn't see him actively asking his friends and relatives to test to see if they were a match. She wanted to know if Martha spurned his advance. Maya asked them not to fight and leave. "Martha isn't an impostor. She was directed in a dream to find her and the other time; the voice again told her to find Maya in the park. Why would anyone risk being called a nut to come find me. I knew her. I saw her on TV news and then on The View. You don't know what you say. I love her. She makes things feel right and if there is a God, and I know there is, he made her give me a kidney. So please leave Dad. Do not come back to see me."

Martha calls Maya. She senses her daughter needs her. The phone rings without an answer. She sends a text asking if she is alright; to call or text back. Martha calls again and still no answer. She tells herself not to panic. Maya is in the hospital if there is an emergency. Sharon asks who is calling and tells her to answer because Martha may be worried. She picks up at the other end.

"Everything good? Why didn't you pick up or text? Why are you crying?

"Which answer you need first?"

"Crying."

"Someone. Upset me but I will be okay."

Martha surmises Maya can't talk freely. "Okay honey, take it easy. I am coming with the surprise."

"Alright," said Maya.

"When did dad get so angry and harsh? What made you two stops loving each other? You had date nights and were lovey dovey. Is that midlife crisis? Does it pay to work it out. Look at grandma and grandpa. You should try again. Talk with him because I stay at grandma's permanently."

"Maya, please honey, do not stress and upset yourself. What is to be must be. You know I love your father, but it takes two to talk, listen and reason. But I will try again."

"Thank you, that's all I ask. Love you mom."

"Love you, Maya," said Sharon. She hugs Maya and leaves.

Sasha and the BGs are ready to go but she calls Adrian and explains about Maya and wants the visit with her mother to be perfect, so she's taking a taxi with Sasha to the hospital, and he should come directly there. He reluctantly agrees. And all four take a cab but when they reach the hospital, the Sturgeones left so there's a more pleasant atmosphere. Martha goes to paved the way. Maya is teary eyed and clings to Martha as she explains she sent her dad away asking him not to visit her there. Martha assures her everything is going to be fine. Martha encourages Maya to wash her face to erase evidence of tears and dust some Mary Kay translucent powder on her face and gives her Pink Wink lip gloss. She tells her to put her head tie on as it's part of her surprise. Once finished, Sasha and the boy's visit. The boys compliment her on her looks; she is prettier than last visit. As they all laugh, Martha's phone rings. She listens then tells the boys to say goodbye. As they leave, Martha tells Maya she's going for the surprise, so just sit tight. Moments later, she hears Martha's voice telling someone to be patient. Just a few more step; Maya could not move.

"Okay, mom, this is your surprise. Meet Maya."

"Oh, my Lord. Oh, my Lord. Dorette said. And as she sees Maya in the head tie; It is like looking at herself in the mirror. She starts to cry.

"Yes, mother, your granddaughter, Peter's twin."

"Oh grandmother, you do look like me." She hugs and kisses her grandmother. The best surprise ever." She runs and kisses Martha and goes back to her grandmother.

"You look like me young lady. You even wear the same lips gloss." And they look at each other and laugh. The nurse pokes her head in to find reason for the jubilation.

"Did you tell her husband to come pick her up? Because they are going to ignore us, won't miss us and won't see us."

"Really, honey? Why you say that?" asked Adrian.

"Well, one is my mother, the other my daughter; two peas in a pod. I may look like her, but I am my dad. So, he can have the pleasure of separating those two. Watch this. Mom. Mom, Maya. Maya, we're leaving. Mom, we are leaving, said Martha. She is ignored, so she kisses Maya on the head and her mother's cheek, but she knows they didn't see her. Like I said, we won't be missed."

"Well, gorgeous, you can lavish your attention on me. I would never, ever ignore you." And kisses her deeply. As he raises his head and looks in her eyes around of cheer goes up and they walk out hand in hand. When they reached home the elastic from her pants tore off the cover from her cut. It is healing but has a way to go. Stitches should disintegrate as it heals. She will find the dressings from here on. She asks Adrian to put the post-surgical tape on. She tells him she's tired and wants to sleep. She uses wet wipes on arms, and torso and then finds a house dress. She dreams of Peter who opposes the visit? She talks them into one visit. Peter visits the family. Monday morning, she calls the Dunstons and asks if they could meet and talk and compromise. She tells them she doesn't understand anger towards her when her live baby was stolen, and she is presented with a dead child/ their dead child. How do they get to be angry? It is in their interest to be cordial and work with her. Even if there are documents, she never signed anything, and the Judge ordered them to tell Peter. She is detracting nothing from them, they raised him. They cared for him. The information will not come from her.

Epilogue

The first official meeting between the Chimes and Dunston took place August 4th. Peter is reluctant to meet. So, al the day before they went out alone, she asked him if he knows the story of Moses in the Bible, Exodus 2: 1-10. And explained she was his mother. But due to circumstances. He was with the Dunstons. But she, the mother, became the babysitter for two years. She did not tell her parents and once she did, they wanted to meet him. Hence meeting in the park with her parents and grandparent, and her siblings. They want to love him and get to know him. Not to be cut off from the people that he has known for years. But he has to get to know the rest of his family. He is a twin. He has a sister, Maya who dying to meet him.

As the families begin to blend and meld, healing, love and forgiveness abounds. The twins are excited to be together. Ogwin has a family now and is not very interested in being a part of the blend, but his sister Jill visits and renews her friendship with Martha.

The Dunstans are gradually coming around. Maternal grandmother and granddaughter are as thick as thieves and Nana's new best friend is Adrian. Dorette loves her son-in-law to be and Nana says he loves her fierce. His eyes follow Marty as Cliff's follow you. With that, Dorette's mission is to see them married soon. Maya continues college the three young men will start college in the fall.

Finally, Adrian pops the question after confessing about investigating her for Dungkirk's death / murder. Once he explained it was to prove she was not involved and after her anger abated, they made up. Adrian wanted to marry immediately but gave her three months and sulked through two of them. They married on December 3rd with watery sunshine and mild weather. She made a radiant bride with WASP bridesmaids and Maya as maid of honor. The BGs formed part of the groomsmen. Adrian's parents, John and Saundra Boone, are delighted with their son's choice, as are his two older brothers, (Shane and Orlando) likewise the two younger sisters, (Geneive and Michelle). They see how happy he is. And the Lord blessed them. They found favor with the Lord and eighteen months later, today is Martha's EDC. This time there is prenatal care, and she is about to prove that lightning doesn't strike the same place twice is a myth. She and Adrian know they are having twins. All he talks about is his daughters. You don't know that honey, she'd caution always. "Well, I am hoping why? Because I'll get to make love to you over and over again, because your desire is to give me a son." At 10:35 am on May 29th Rev Martha Renee Boone and Adrian John Boone welcome Saundra Dorette Boone and Adrian John Boone 11 to the family. Exhausted but glowing after her delivery teased, what did you say about your wife's desire for you, something about a son?"

"That the Lord will provide me with a son and daughter. Look honey he did," Adrian said kissing her.

And the family laughed and cheered aware because of his earlier assertion that he'd have daughters. The twins Maya and Peter cheered loudest. Great job mom!

Acknowledgement

To my faithful family of supporters, who encourage me, sweat with me and persevere with me. You are all simply the best; Janett, Lorraine, Fatima, Mike, Dom, Max, Norma, Alzie, Yvonne, Vanessa, Jas, Yoki, Max, Madison, Frederica, Harry and Danny. Thank you so much; always in gratitude into document.

About the Author

As a child author's love for reading blossomed into a passion for storytelling. Despite initially doubting her ability to write a full novel, she created stories, poetry, and prose, inspired by everything from books to radio dramas. After years of writing poetry, she published Ode to Littetrose, a tribute to her mother. Now, in retirement, she fulfills a lifelong dream with her debut novel, Sins of the Parents.

www.ingramcontent.com/pod-product-compliance
Lightning Source LLC
Chambersburg PA
CBHW030322080526
44584CB00012B/669